1ˢᵗ 1925

18901

Arthur Symons

ARTHUR SYMONS.
From a painting by Jacques E. Blanche.

Arthur Symons

A Critical Study

by T. Earle Welby

Author of "A Popular History of English Poetry,"
"Figs from Thistles," etc.

London : A. M. Philpot, Ltd.
69 Great Russell Street, W.C.
1925

[Copyright.]

*Printed in Great Britain by Hazell, Watson & Viney, Ld.,
London and Aylesbury.*

To

DORA

CONTENTS

ILLUSTRATIONS

I

A PRELIMINARY VIEW

IT is not as the most considerable poet of his generation, for he is not quite that, nor is it as its finest critic, though he is that, but as a writer unique in his by now almost completely realised ambition that I propose to deal with Mr. Arthur Symons. There is nothing in his work, or in the man as I know him, to suggest that he ever condescended to the vulgarity of competition ; and in writing of him I beg to be excused from attempts to justify treatment of his writings on this scale by claiming for him any particular place among his contemporaries in this or that department of literature. So far as I can gather, few judges would, to-day, place him so high as a poet as I should, and few would deny him pre-eminence as a critic ; but I am not much concerned to convert those who, as I think, undervalue his poetry, or to point to corroboration when I applaud his criticism. What I am anxious to do is to secure consideration of his work as a whole, and, through that, recognition of an achievement which, be it at any particular point greater or less than I take it to be, is assuredly without true contemporary parallel.

To me, and I will dare to guess to himself, Mr. Arthur Symons is not the author of certain poems, poetic plays, criticisms, imaginary portraits, evocations of the souls of cities, but a writer who, not in mere versatility, but with a fixed purpose in choosing many media, has gradually worked out a complete system of æsthetics, has gradually fashioned a whole imaginative world of his own. For mere convenience, one may deal with his work in verse apart from his criticism, but the poet is only half, and indeed as it happens less than half, of this man, and the critic, though he may well be honoured for his frequent success in the ordinary task of a critic, cannot be rightly estimated if we forget that his work is complementary to that of the poet.

All of his work might be called critical, all of it might be called creative ; it is all a testing of the arts of man, and of the art of God in the visible beauty of the earth, by certain invariable principles, and the co-ordination of all that responds to those principles, under a single system of æsthetics, into a world of his own. His criticism is his means of escaping from the limits of his strictly and directly creative power as a poet. One hemisphere

2

he has made as a poet, the other he makes over again as a critic, completing his world ; it is that world we have ultimately to judge.

Intelligent people, quite sympathetic, but a little surprised that one should talk so much in the nineteen-twenties of a writer of the eighteen-nineties, have said to me that Mr. Symons has written no single poem superior to, or even equal to, the finest poem of this or that writer of what they call his period ; and sometimes they have suggested that this consummate critic of literature has written less well of painting or of the theatre or of music than some contemporary specialist. They may be right. They are certainly wrong when they hint that this alternation of obviously creative and apparently only critical effort, and this attempt to deal not only with literature but with painting, sculpture, architecture, music, acting, dancing, and with the character and atmosphere of cities and sea-coasts, is but the work of a discreeter and technically more accomplished, humanly less interesting John Addington Symonds. All this work, though I do not say every single thing in every department of it, has been necessary. All of it has a place, else empty, in the working out of the writer's system.

I say working out, with intention. The principles implicit in the poems are not propounded in the criticism with the writers and artists nominally under treatment as excuse. It is the distinction of this critic that his first duty, that to his subject, is discharged scrupulously, his private and remoter purpose being served without any special pleading, his peculiar part of the truth emerging as the whole truth is disengaged. He is not an abstract thinker ; he is an artist ; and caring only for first principles, cares for them only when they are made flesh, but—which is the point—whether by himself or by the incarnating imagination of another, whom he will criticise, matters hardly at all to his true purpose.

Consider those imaginary portraits, they are scarcely stories, which are entitled *Spiritual Adventures*. It is mere chance they come to us as creative work, the chance that no novelist offered him anything like those morbid temperaments. Had some writer of fiction done so, Mr. Symons, I am confident, would have felt none of the despair of the novelist who finds himself anticipated. He would still have been able to do what matters most to him, and in a way to which he is more accustomed, as a critic. The persons in *Spiritual Adventures* are so many pairs of eyes for looking at the beauty and curiosity of the world, and necessary to Mr. Symons because, since " the eye altering alters all," certain aspects can be seen only by looking at them as if through the eyes of another person. To

4

have first to create that other person, instead of finding him in Balzac or Stendhal or Gabriele d'Annunzio or some other, is a task to which this critic can rise, but it is imposed by the negligence of novelists rather than by a need in himself which could only be satisfied by the creative act.

His evidently creative work, in the poems, deals very unusually often with works of art, and with the highly artificial though unintended beauty of the modern urban landscape, the creative energy being exercised on material which has already been far removed from the simplicity of nature, shaped to an artist's ideal or teased and it may be corrupted by the demands on it of the multitude. He is very largely a poet of the artificial, and will sometimes reduce nature to mere illustration of the artificial, as in the really beautiful second stanza of a poem on the rouge and powder on a woman's face :

> *Gracile and creamy white and rose,*
> *Complexioned like the flower of dawn,*
> *Her fleeting colours are as those*
> *That, from an April sky withdrawn,*
> *Fade in a fragrant mist of tears away*
> *When weeping noon° leads on the altered day.*

It is not that he objects to nature. He could from the first appreciate certain aspects of her, and he came in time to have a very individual and pathetic feeling for her. But nature, in his early poems, ſtirs him only where it is an intruder among artificial things. He valued her, as Swinburne said of Baudelaire, on those sides on which nature seems moſt unnatural.

The orchid moſtly is the flower I love,
And violets, the mere violets of the wood,
For all their sweetness, have not power to move
The curiosity that rules my blood.

Yet here, in this spice-laden atmosphere,
Where only nature is a thing unreal,
I found in juſt a violet, planted here,
The artificial flower of my ideal.

The attitude, it has often enough been said, of a decadent poet. And certainly in the earlier poems, with their frequent perversity in choice of subject or in treatment, there are many pieces and passages only a poet of the decadence, not quite the same thing as a decadent poet, could have written. But the comparison with Baudelaire has usually been as unilluminating as the comparison, far less reasonable on a general view of the work of Mr. Symons, with Verlaine. Mr. Symons, less human, less impulsive than Verlaine, is altogether more important as a general artiſtic intelligence than the

6

greater poet. In being both poet and critic, and in working with fixed principles, he is very much more like Baudelaire. Yet, in the widespread and probably incorrigible misunderstanding of Baudelaire, for which Mr. Symons himself, though understanding Baudelaire very well, has unfortunately given excuse, there could hardly be a worse service to the English writer than to compare him with the French. That Mr. Symons at one time devoted many poems to recording the sensations procured by frequent change of sleeping accommodation and company, and has always been ready to write of questionable interiors, artificial paradises, bought dreams, and the snake-like and feline elements in feminine human nature, does not really much matter. What justifies a comparison with Baudelaire is that Mr. Symons possesses, though he uses it otherwise than the great masters, the power of organising all his material, a power which only Baudelaire of the poets of the decadence has had. It is far from obvious in Mr. Symons. He has written few poems of any length, fewer of any complexity, and may easily be taken for nothing more than a poet of moods and impressions. But regard his work as a whole, the criticism supplementing the poems, and you become aware that, though most of his poems are slight and most of his critical work is made up of short essays each on a single figure, what you finally have from it is an organised world.

Were there in any important quarter to-day a disposition to overvalue Mr. Symons, it might be my duty to point out at some length that this world is rather lacking in vital warmth. In his own way Mr. Symons has warmed both hands before the fire of life, or, rather, before certain fastidiously chosen portions of it, but as a poet he usually seems to be remembering the heat instead of writing out of the actual sensation of it. Meaning a little more for this reason to those who accumulate emotional and æsthetic experiences for the pleasure of retrospect, he means the less to people in general, who, if they want poetry at all, want it to be struck off immediately from the poet's experience. And there are other reservations that it might, in other circumstances, be necessary to make. It would be wrong to say that Mr. Symons as a poet is not interested in humanity, but his interest in it is one of curiosity rather than sympathy, the interest of one who is not himself on the whole very human in creatures in many respects so differently constituted. I find it significant in him as a man that he likes walking alone through crowds, and has chosen to travel abroad so much ; he is as a poet almost always the solitary observer in the throng, and all men are in a sense foreigners to him. A limitation, of course,

8

but not without advantages, since he takes hardly
anything for granted in human conduct, and pre-
serves a capacity for part naïve, part malicious
surprise over what would be commonplace to
anyone quite a native of the world.

The poet, however, as I have already suggested,
though the essential part of this writer, is less than
half of him. Turn to the criticism, and you are
at once aware of a broadening of the writer's interests. If he had produced no line of criticism,
you might excusably, judging from most of his
poetry, have doubted whether he could be a critic
of the supreme masters and other broadly human
artists. Mallarmé, Jules Laforgue, the Whistler of
the minor etchings and lithographs, Aubrey Beardsley, yes ; but surely not Shakespeare, Balzac,
Beethoven, Rodin. Well, the complete, quietly
triumphant refutation is before you in page after
page of the most divining criticism of just those
great masters. Those very human qualities which
as a poet he seemed either to ignore or to have only
a changeling's curiosity about are now fully appreciated, and even in work on a lower level, about
the strict artistic value of which he is rightly
doubtful, as when he praises Lamb's poem, " The
Old Familiar Faces," for its wonderful raw
humanity. It would seem that anything to which
as a man, that is, as a poet, he is unresponsive, or

9

about which he is only curious from without, has only to be presented to him in a work of art for his response to be faultless and intimate. The critic completes the poet. But then the critic would be little more than a man of fine taste and wide reading if the poet were not there to aid with a profound and subtle intuition. Creative and critical, the work of Mr. Symons must be considered as a whole, though for the humble purposes of this pedestrian survey I now proceed to separate it, hoping to bring it together again for judgment in my concluding chapter.

II

THE EARLY POEMS

MR. ARTHUR SYMONS was born on the 28th February 1865, in Wales, of Cornish parentage. He was educated at various private schools, but was, I understand, largely self-taught, acquiring, for example, his knowledge of the living foreign languages by constant reading of versions of the Bible in those languages.

He knew no settled home in boyhood, being thus, as he says, cut off from whatever is stable and of long growth in the world. No profession or business was ever seriously contemplated for him or by him ; he turned to literature, without, at that time, any sense of having anything particular to say, merely to set up a barrier of books between himself and people in general. Finding himself slowly, he became in the late 'eighties and early 'nineties a frequent contributor to the *Academy*, the *Athenæum*, the *Saturday Review*, and other periodicals. He was one of those who made the books of the Rhymers' Club, where Dowson, Lionel Johnson, and Mr. Yeats were among his associates ; he contributed to the *Yellow Book*, and, with Aubrey Beardsley, edited the more significant *Savoy*. Something more than the restlessness of the man, the instinct of the artist in search of his material, made him a traveller. Paris, Rome, Venice, Seville, and other cities drew him. London, in which he lived long in Fountain Court, remained his headquarters till he settled, more definitely than one would have thought likely, at Wittersham, in Kent, twenty years ago. His companions in art, with the almost solitary exception of Mr. Yeats, died before he or they had reached forty, and he entered this century a somewhat lonely figure.

His principal works in verse are : *Days and Nights*, 1889 ; *Silhouettes*, 1892 ; *London Nights*, 1894 ; *Amoris Victima*, 1897 ; *Images of Good and Evil*, 1901 ; *A Book of Twenty Songs*, 1905 ; *The Fool of the World*, 1907 ; *Knave of Hearts*, 1913 ; and the poetic dramas, *Tragedies*, 1916 ; *Tristan and Iseult*, 1917. His collected poems appeared in 1902.

In prose he has published : *An Introduction to the Study of Browning*, 1886 ; *Studies in Two Literatures*, 1897, subsequently broken up to provide part of the contents of *Studies in Prose and Verse*, 1904, and *Studies in Elizabethan Drama*, 1920 ; *The Symbolist Movement in Literature*, 1899 ; *Plays, Acting and Music*, 1903 ; *Cities*, 1903 ; *Spiritual Adventures*, 1905 ; *Studies in Seven Arts*, 1906 ; *William Blake*,

12

1907; *The Romantic Movement in English Poetry*, 1909; *Figures of Several Centuries*, 1916; with other volumes of less importance.

Besides making the almost matchless versions from Verlaine, Mallarmé, and others, included amongst his own poems, he has translated "Les Aubes," by Verhaeren, the "Electra" of Hoffman-stahl, the "Petits Poèmes en Prose" of Baudelaire, the "Dead City," "Francesca da Rimini," and "Gioconda" of Gabriele d' Annunzio, and the incidental poems in the same writer's novel, "The Child of Pleasure."

An apparently not quite complete, though at one or two points rather too generously inclusive, "Collected Edition of the Works of Arthur Symons" is now in process of publication. It is in sixteen volumes in a style to which this book conforms.

The largest collection of his manuscripts and first editions, that formed by Mr. Quin, of New York, was lately dispersed on the sale of that bibliophile's library.

The dedication of his books, to Meredith, whom, however, he never met, to Walter Pater, to Verlaine, to Mr. W. B. Yeats, to Mr. Hardy, to Maeterlinck, to Joseph Conrad, record some of his chief admirations and friendships. To these names should be added those of Mallarmé, Coventry Patmore,

Ernest Dowson, Mr. Augustus John, Eleanora
Duse, Yvette Guilbert, Pachmann, Mr. Havelock
Ellis.

Another dedication, that prefixed to *Studies in
Seven Arts*, states part of his intellectual obligation
to his wife, whom he married in 1901 : " You
have a far clearer sense than I have of the special
qualities, the special limits, of the various arts. . . .
In my endeavour to master what I have called the
universal science of beauty, I owe more to you than
to technical books or to technical people ; because
in you there is some hardly conscious instinct which
turns towards beauty unerringly, like the magnet,
at the attraction of every vital current."

The earliest verses he can remember writing were
some lines, natural enough as the work of the child
of so pious a house, entitled, " The Lord is Good."
These he produced at the age of nine. At thirteen,
he wrote some Byronic tales in verse, some lyric
pieces, and, already the poet of bought dreams, a
piece on opium. A little later, at Tiverton and
Bideford, he set himself to the imitation of Tennyson,
of Browning, and of Swinburne. In 1880, on his
fifteenth birthday, he produced a monologue,
" Mad," which he thinks had a certain vigour,
and in the latter half of that year there was a marked
development in his work, chiefly under the influence
of Swinburne, one of whose French lyrics he about

14

that time translated. Versions from Schiller, from Heine, from Aristophanes, from the Provençal, and a rendering of the first 330 lines of the " Prometheus Bound," followed. He wrote also, before his seventeenth year, a long lyric, which he condemns as vague but describes as possessing atmosphere, " On the River," and " The Defence of Delilah," in twenty-five stanzas of true *terza rima*, done under the influence of Leconte de Lisle, with which may have mingled, one suspects, that of William Morris.

His study of the Elizabethan dramatists must have begun very early. He was qualified, when hardly out of boyhood, to edit the Shakespeare facsimiles issued by Quaritch, and it is a veteran of scholarship in this sort who addresses us in, for example, the admirable pages on John Day, written when he was only twenty-four. But there is, except in method, equal maturity in the *Introduction to the Study of Browning*, written before he was twenty-one, and still, at any rate in its revised form, the best preparation for Browning.

Dykes Campbell, the editor of Coleridge, was his counsellor when he was writing on Browning. The volume was reviewed with a discreet generosity in the *Guardian* by Walter Pater, whose friendship Mr. Symons had gained, whose influence was strong upon him, and who was the most encouraging critic

15

of the first volume of poetry, *Days and Nights*, published by Mr. Symons.

Some of the pieces in *Days and Nights* date back to 1884, the nineteenth year of their author's life; and we have seen how early was the development of his critical faculty. A precocious writer, one would say; but no, and for a reason deserving full statement.

In one of his critical studies, Mr. Symons has suggested that Gabriele d'Annunzio, whom he justly appreciates, and from whom he has made remarkable translations, is wholly dependent on visual and other physical promptings and sensual experiences, and with dim eyes or in a monk's cell might have written nothing. Well, Mr. Symons as a poet is almost entirely dependent on sight, on the memory of delicate physical sensations, on a rich, fastidiously discriminated æsthetic experience. This man sees more, where he cares to look at all, with those fine eyes, than any other man I have known. The interior of a café, the ballet, which I have seen with him, the face of a man or woman introduced to him, the binding of a book, anything with the promise of interest to him, he absorbs with a concentrated, disinterested lust of the eyes, getting everything out of it, storing away the precise image of the thing when it is not, as it mostly will be, something which disappoints him. When he was writing his early poems Mr. Symons had simply not seen enough of the things that mean most to him. He had not yet discovered what the ballet held for his eyes ; he had not seen Paris, Venice, Rome, Seville ; and though he was writing, in 1884, lines for a picture by Burne-Jones, and even, nearer his future subjects, for a design by Félicien Rops, he had not yet begun to see in pictures what he found when, in 1889, he wrote the equivalent of a picture by Watteau, much less what he found, in 1899, when he transposed a fan by Charles Conder with this exquisite felicity :

Beauty I love, yet more than this I love
Beautiful things ; and, more than love, delight ;
Colours that faint ; dim echo far above
The crystal sound, and shadow beyond sight.

For I am tired with youth and happiness
As other men are tired with age and grief ;
This is to me a longer weariness :
Sadly I ask of each sad mask relief.

For gardens where I know not if I find
Autumn or spring about the shadowy fruit,
Or if it is the sighing of the wind
Or if it is the sighing of the lute.

He had not, when *Days and Nights* appeared, even begun to utilise, in the way proper to him, that spectacle which his eyes, for some two or three

C

years, had been devouring insatiably, with a minute curiosity, the great spectacle of London.

" If ever there was a religion of the eyes," he has written, with reference to his first years in London, " I have devoutly practised that religion. I noted every face that passed me on the pavement; I looked into the omnibuses, the cabs, always with the same eager hope of seeing some beautiful or interesting person, some gracious movement, a delicate expression, which would be gone if I did not catch it as it went. This search without an aim grew to be almost a torture to me; my eyes ached with the effort, but I could not control them. At every moment, I knew, some spectacle awaited them; I grasped at all these sights with the same futile energy as a dog that I once saw standing in an Irish stream, and snapping at the bubbles that continually passed him on the water. Life ran past me continually, and I tried to make all its bubbles my own."

But Mr. Symons, as he has himself explained, is one of those who can utilise impressions only when they have long been brooded over.

> *My singing-time has not begun*
> *While I can say it is the day,*
> *For I am idle in the sun*
> *Until the sun has passed away.*

The Early Poems

And then I turn and look within
As the world vanishes from me,
And in my twilight brain I spin
These cobwebs out of memory.

When he was writing the pieces in his first volume
he had either not encountered his true subjects or
had not travelled far enough past experience for
retrospect to be natural. And it was for this
reason, more than any other, that the book held
a good deal not really characteristic.

Technically, if by technique is meant knowledge
of one's materials rather than of one's special task,
the volume was mature enough. The command
of rhythm is already evident :

One sighs, for I have seen the privet pale,
The roses perish and the lilies fail.

Evident, too, is competence in bringing off certain
traditional effects, such as that which rounds and
gives weight to the last words of a sonnet, " The
Nun " :

Yet ineradicably deep
Hides in her heart an alien Paradise.

Everywhere there is lucidity, and in the dramatic
and narrative pieces there is a firm grasp on motive.
But Mr. Symons at that time had submitted some-

what incautiously to the influence of Browning,
an influence felt in his mature work only as it has
helped him to write some of the most truly vocal
verse of our time, but then responsible for a rather
crude dramatic realism.   Yet, perhaps, it is less
Browning than some nameless editor of a " Complete Reciter " who must be blamed for " Red
Bredbury's End," " The Knife-Thrower," " Mar-
gery of the Fens," and only the fact that Wilde's
boyish melodrama, " Vera," was then unpublished
holds me from suspecting that it had something
to do with the origin of "An Episode under the
Nihilists."   It is not that these things, and still
less that "A Revenge," " Bell in Camp," and "An
Interruption in Court " are ineffectual.   Each makes
its point.   But such things belong, essentially,
to a category in which Robert Buchanan was
occasionally almost a master, not to that in which
genuine dramatic lyrics fall.   Nevertheless here
and there even in some of these pieces, but far
more in such a sonnet as " The Opium-Smoker,"
we are aware of the poet who emerged in 1892,
in the volume entitled *Silhouettes*.

How are we to explain the difference between
these poems and those dated only three or four
years earlier ?   My argument would explain it
by increase of the peculiar experience needed by
this poet almost for his existence as an achieving

poet, and by a lapse of time permitting earlier experience to become matter for retrospect. And that, indeed, I take to be the main part of the explanation. But there are other considerations which should not be ignored. Mr. Symons had not only acquainted himself with the ballet, with the work of certain painters, with certain foreign scenes. He had largely escaped from the domination of Browning, to come under the spell of Verlaine, and he had begun to subtilise his technique.

Questions of technique go deeper than people in general understand, or, understanding, are quite willing to allow. The popular conception of a poet is of one who, labouring with ideas and under emotion, eventually finds a technique for their expression. But technical development often comes first, and often influences choice from among the many subjects which have stirred thought and feeling in the writer. Mr. Symons, with new material, with some older material at length ready for him to work upon, must frequently have chosen or rejected a subject by reference to its fitness for the tenuous, more purely lyrical, more impressionistic verse he began to write about 1890.

Almost everything requiring statement or elaboration was now banished by him. The aim was now, with the utmost economy, to suggest momentary impressions, transient moods ; the impressions to

be, by preference, those of one gazing at things
themselves artificial or seen under an artificial light,
the moods to be not only fleeting but frivolous or
perverse. And in this endeavour Mr. Symons,
it can hardly be necessary to remind any likely
reader, secured from time to time a delicate success.
If you look at some of the best of these *Silhouettes*,
and even more if you turn to the maturer *London
Nights*, which followed in 1895, with a dedication
to Verlaine, you will find certain small difficult
things, of a real novelty, done with a rare skill.
Certain effects of colour, which might have been
brushed off a moth's wings and which the first
breath will scatter ; certain movements, of a dancer
seen perhaps from the wings ; certain notes of a
just audible music ; certain moods which flutter
through the mind and are gone, have been seized
delicately, firmly, and perpetuated without any of
that incongruous mason's art which too often
mars the propriety of " a moment's monument."
Many of the pieces are very slight, some only just
exist : a faint dust of colour, a mere breath of music
issuing reluctantly from silence and swooning back
into it. But let us not deceive ourselves into under-
valuation, or into the less probable error of over-
valuation. As Mr. Symons himself has pointed
out, in an early essay in praise of Henley, it is easy
to mistake obviously matter-full, eloquent verse, in

FOUNTAIN COURT, THE TEMPLE, WHERE PAUL VERLAINE STAYED WITH ARTHUR SYMONS.

which nothing essential is done, for poetry, and even easier to esteem too lightly the inspiration in verse which catches a passing impulse, an evanescent sensation. A six-foot canvas on which a landscape with all its details is rendered, accurately, with taste, is not necessarily a finer thing, nor even proof of greater industry, than some " song on stone " by Whistler. No ; and we may well be willing to sacrifice a score of thoughtful, eloquent sonnets on the usual subjects for one of these slight, rather frivolous, rather perverse pieces by Mr. Symons, whether it be that in which the Javanese dancers live for us—

> *While the gnats of music whirr*
> *The little amber-coloured dancers move,*
> *Like painted idols seen to stir*
> *By the idolators in a magic grove—*

or that in which the negation of colour comes to us with the ghost of music—

> *White girl, your flesh is lilies*
> *Under a frozen moon,*
> *So still is*
> *The rapture of your swoon*
> *Of whiteness, snow or lilies—*

or in that in which the verse revolves for La Mélinite, exquisite and ambiguous flower of evil, to the

23

Strains of Olivier Metra's Waltz of Roses. And
there are two or three pure songs, with no burden
but that of their music, which seem to me even
finer :

> *Her eyes say Yes, her lips say No.*
> *Ah, tell me, Love, when she denies*
> *Shall I believe the lips or eyes ?*
> *Bid eyes no more dissemble,*
> *Or lips too tremble*
> *The way her heart would go !*

A trifle of two stanzas, in expression of nothing
more important than a light lover's agreeable
suspense, but look through the anthologies and
see how many songs, outside the Elizabethans',
can be matched against it.

All the same, when Mr. Symons was writing
such things he occasionally forgot, as a poet, a
truth admitted and in fact emphasised by him as a
critic. In a Preface to the second edition of
Silhouettes, he wrote, in 1896 :

"I do not wish to assert that the kind of verse
which happened to reflect certain moods of mine
at a certain period of my life is the best kind of
verse in itself, or is likely to seem to me, in other
years, when other moods may have made me their
own, the best kind of verse for my own expression
of myself. Nor do I affect to doubt that the crea-

24

tion of the supreme emotion is a higher form of art than the reflection of the most exquisite sensation, the evocation of the most magical impression."

And in a criticism of the painting of Watts, written in 1900, he said :

"Whistler tricks life and the world into beauty by accepting in them only what suits his purpose, as indeed every artist must do, but also by narrowing his purpose until it is indeed, for the most part, aptly symbolised by the butterfly of his signature."

Mr. Symons, in the early and middle 'nineties, for the most part narrowed his purpose as a poet until, to an ungenerous eye, he seemed concerned only with the most fragile, the most ephemeral impressions and moods. That frailty of subject necessarily means frailty in the poem expressive of it is, of course, the belief only of the stupid, and it must be acknowledged that in some of the slightest poems of this writer the slenderness is only that of an artist in fine wrought-iron work. But as Whistler, after all, is a great, instead of only an exquisite artist, by virtue of the Carlyle and the portrait of his mother, so Mr. Symons is a considerable poet by virtue of later and broader work than any we have yet glanced at.

Some promise of the later work is evident in the second and third of his volumes of verse. He had written, as early as 1891, in the piece entitled

"On Judges' Walk," a poem which escapes out
of the region in which observant eyes, sensitive
nerves, and a gift for delicate cadence suffice. It
is a poem of reticence, and it is brief, simple, without any surprising felicity of phrase; but some
miracle has been worked, and it is big with things
of tremendous import which will never be said.
There is another poem, utterly different, with a
beautiful use of an artifice of repetition much
favoured by Mr. Symons, which deals with something more permanent than impressions and moods.
I mean that piece, one of its author's chief lyrical
successes, which forms the eighth of the series
entitled "Bianca." If you consider its structure,
with the repetition of words in the penultimate
line of each stanza, the recurrence of the rhyme
word of the first line in each stanza in a lengthened
participial form at the end of the third line, it is as
artificial as verse can be; only the artifice remains
unsuspected, appears the most natural thing in
the world.

With the "Bianca" poems we are in the garden
of *fleurs du mal*. Mr. Symons found it necessary
in the 'nineties to deal with charges of immorality
directed against many of the pieces in *London
Nights*, and did so in a preface, afterwards reprinted
in *Studies in Prose and Verse*, to the second edition
of the volume. I do not know that, at this time

of day, we need revive that controversy. But the
present writer feels a certain purely literary objection
to these pieces in the mass, though admiring some
of them individually. It is possible, after all, to
make a little too much fuss, on this side as well as
on the other, about what Chamfort called the
contact of two epidermes, and a catalogue of light
loves and temporary domesticities needs ingenuity
and the salt of cynicism if it is to escape some tinge
of the ridiculous. So far as these pieces are impressions of things seen, I have nothing to urge
against them. Only Henley, in a few of his
hospital poems, has done interiors better than the
author of

> *The little bedroom papered red,*
> *The gas's faint malodorous light,*

and of :

> *The feverish room and that white bed,*
> *The tumbled skirts upon a chair,*
> *The novel flung half-open where*
> *Hat, hair-pins, puffs, and paints are spread . . .*

> *And you half-dressed and half awake,*
> *Your slant eyes strangely watching me,*
> *And I, who watch you drowsily,*
> *With eyes that, having slept not, ache ;*

27

> *This (need one dread? nay dare one hope?)*
> *Will rise, a ghost of memory, if*
> *Ever again my handkerchief*
> *Is scented with white heliotrope.*

But the irregularity of the situation adds nothing to its interest, and poems of this sort might have been produced without postulating frailty in the poet's imagined companion.

These things, and even some in which sin is a necessary part of the subject, are open, I think, to an objection quite other than the ordinary moralist's—the objection that they are *not* flowers of evil at all. It is paying too much of a compliment at once to conventional virtue and conventional vice to emphasise a " fall " which leaves the stumbler on precisely the same level as before. Sin with remorse or exultation is one thing, and matter for great poetry ; sin without either is quite another. Great poetry can celebrate the transcending of sex or the vehement assertion of it, but can hardly be expected to hymn a mere change of bed-fellow. Unless, indeed, the intellect can be induced to play on the situation with irony or casuistical defence. And, personally, I could wish that Mr. Symons, who has so sensitively generous an appreciation of Rochester, and in his really impassioned work can sometimes compete in casuistry with

Donne, had oftener treated light, irregular love, to dignify it by that name, in the spirit of his only cynical song :

> *May we not love as others do,*
> *Dearest, because we love,*
> *A mistress I, a husband you ?*
> *Nay, our delights must prove*
> *Either the double or the part*
> *Of those who love with single heart . . .*
>
> *Both spare and prodigal were we,*
> *To love but you, to love but me.*

Still, with one of the " Bianca " poems, I suppose to the moralist the most offensive, the intellect has begun to work, and on a situation which really would have interested such great poets as Baudelaire and Swinburne. And something else has happened in this philosophising of a morbid content-in-discontent : Mr. Symons has discovered his absolute command of the octosyllabic couplet, with which, whenever he has since chosen to use it, he has done whatever he willed. The poem is the utterance of a man who, having loved almost sexlessly, and then, in despair, turned to the easy certainties of bought love—

> *Only the good firm flesh to hold,*
> *The love well worth its weight in gold,*

29

has wearied of that :

> *But that too palled and I began*
> *To find that man was mostly man*
> *In that, his will being sated, he*
> *Wills ever new variety.*

And so he has finally given himself to a love or lust that deliberately, perversely, denies itself its ultimate expression, teases sense with a corrupt asceticism, pauses on the very verge of too obvious a bliss.

> *Ambiguous child, whose life retires*
> *Into the pulse of those desires*
> *Of whose endured possession speaks*
> *The passionate pallor of your cheeks ;*
> *Child, in whom neither good nor ill*
> *Can sway your sick and swaying will,*
> *Only the aching sense of sex*
> *Wholly controls, and does perplex,*
> *With dubious drifts scarce understood,*
> *The shaken currents of your blood ;*
> *It is your ambiguity*
> *That speaks to me and conquers me,*
> *Your swooning heats of sensual bliss,*
> *Under my hands, under my kiss,*
> *And your strange reticences, strange*
> *Concessions, your illusive change,*

The strangeness of your smile, the faint
Corruption of your gaze, a saint
Such as Luini loved to paint.

What's virtue, Bianca? nay, indeed,
What's vice? for I at last am freed,
With you, of virtue and of vice :
I have discovered Paradise.
And Paradise is neither heaven,
Where the spirits of God are seven,
And the spirits of men burn pure,
Nor is it hell, where souls endure
An equal ecstacy of fire,
In like repletion of desire ;
Nay, but a subtlier intense
Unsatisfied appeal of sense,
Ever desiring, ever near,
The goal of all its hope and fear,
Ever a hair's-breadth from the goal.

So Bianca satisfies my soul.

There, if the shocked reader has followed him
so far, reading of the poetry of Mr. Symons seems
to end. He was labelled early, judged prematurely,
and there persists, among quite intelligent people,
an idea of him as no more than the author of the

poems we have been considering. A poet of impressions and moods, a poet of the brief English decadence in which the *Yellow Book* and the *Savoy* appeared : very definitely dated, people will tell one. Well, for me, at least, the poetry of Mr. Symons almost begins where for such people it ends ; and in the next two sections of this critical study I propose to sketch his development from the moment when a recognisably human passion entered into the little world of alcoves and absinthe, ballet girls, Juliets of a night, things seen as well as they can be seen with the eyes alone, things felt only with the nerves of a delicate but not a noble delight. I admire certain of the earlier poems as much as anyone can ; I see, it is to be hoped, the skill in some of the poems I do not much admire ; and I admit that *London Nights* contains the most novel part of Mr. Symons's contribution to English poetry. But that this sometimes in a sense almost trivial work, remarkable as the best of it is for novelty and skill, should be taken for his whole contribution, while some of the most subtle, passionate, memory-haunted poems of our time should be neglected, is to me an absurdity of a very offensive kind. It is not as the author of *Silhouettes* or of *London Nights* that Mr. Symons joins, if only to occupy the most modest place, those few poets, Donne, the Meredith of " Modern Love," the

32

Patmore of a few poems, the Swinburne of fewer, who have escaped alike from English sentimentality and the divine illusions of love to tell the inner truth about a passion to be endured rather than enjoyed.

III

MODERN LOVE

IN English poetry, for the most part, love is an affair of honest sentiment. That it can turn against itself is but rarely admitted in a poetry reluctant to strike the note of *odi et amo*. Its doubts are seldom of itself, or torturing ; the lover does but doubt whether his love will be returned, whether he is worthy of love. That love may be a kind of insanity or sickness, that it may be an inverted hate or a treacherous truce between opponents indispensable to each other, are ideas as unusual with us as they are usual with the poets of Latin countries. We have a great deal of love poetry, amongst the most beautiful in the world, but it does not occur to an anthologist of it to include in a selection that poem, the " Tired Memory," of Coventry Patmore, which is the most courageously truthful treatment of fidelity in love that we have ; and if you talk about love poetry to ordinary English people, it will probably be some while before the name of Donne is mentioned. Yet the maladies of love, and its cruelty, have had

34

poets with us: Shakespeare in certain of the sonnets; Donne eminently; the Meredith of "Modern Love"; Patmore at times, for all his air of being the apologist of domesticity; Swinburne, though love comes to him chiefly as cerebral excitement, with the metres throbbing in his head; Mr. Symons. A very few other poets might be partially brought in: Browning in a way; Rossetti in a way; more pertinently, the less familiar Keats.

In a criticism of Keats in *The Romantic Movement in English Poetry*, Mr. Symons has written:

"Have you ever thought of the frightful thing it is to shift one's centre? That is what it is to love a woman. One's nature no longer radiates freely from its own centre, the centre itself is shifted, is put outside one's self. Up to then one may have been unhappy, one may have failed, many things may have seemed to have gone wrong. But at least there was this security; that one's enemies were all outside the gate. With the woman one loves one admits all one's enemies. Think: all one's happiness to depend upon the will of another, on that other's fragility, faith, mutability; on the way life comes to the heart, soul, conscience, nerves of someone else, no longer the quite sufficient difficulties of a personal heart, soul, conscience, and nerves. It is to call in a passing stranger and to say: Guard all my treasures while

I sleep, for there is no certainty in the world beyond the certainty that I am I, and that what is not I can never draw one breath for me, though I were dying for lack of it."

Turn to Mr. Symons's verse and you will find the equivalent of this passage of prose.

> *My love makes me afraid,*
> *For when I am alone,*
> *My fate being my own,*
> *I have all myself in aid.*
>
> *But with yourself you bring*
> *Fear, and he will not quit*
> *So dear and exquisite*
> *And perishable a thing . . .*

And again, in " An Epilogue to Love " :

> *You are the world ; I take*
> *My foe into my keeping for your sake . . .*
> *I have loved life for other women's sake,*
> *And now for your sake fear it.*

Look at the last of the *Spiritual Adventures* and you will see, through the highly morbid temperament predicated there, how love comes as an almost intolerable thing to the one who feels himself being minutely taken possession of by a tyranny not the less tyrannical for being benevolent. Of such fears and impotent rebellions, as of the doubts, desperate casuistries, acrid revulsions of love, Mr. Symons, in much of his maturest work, is the poet.

And he is very largely the poet of love remembered. Sight and memory count for almost as much in his poetry as in the otherwise utterly different poetry of Wordsworth. It is not only that he looks back on old experience, actual or imaginary. When the present, one would suppose, would be most absorbing, he is found projecting himself years forward in order to be able to gaze back at it. The present is appreciated as it will be when it is the past. As in some verses of light love already quoted he values the situation not for what it is, but for what it will be in retrospect when a perfume will call it up, so he can hardly praise a woman's beauty until he supposes himself to be recalling it years later.

> *When I am old, and think of the old days,*
> *And warm my hands before a little blaze,*
> *Having forgotten love, hope, fear, desire,*
> *I shall see, smiling out of the pale fire,*
> *One face, mysterious and exquisite . . .*
> *And I shall think of you as something strange,*
> *And beautiful, and full of helpless change,*
> *Which I beheld and carried in my heart ;*
> *But you, I loved, will have become a part*

Of the eternal mystery, and love
Like a dim pain ; and I shall bend above
My little fire, and shiver, being cold,
When you are no more young, and I am old.

Love, with this poet, is almost always the " desire of things unborn or things long dead " :

O heart, hold fast the present.   Then to me
My heart : What is the present ? There is none.
Has not the sigh after the kiss begun
The future ? And the past was in the kiss.
Then to my heart I said : O heart, if this
Be life, then what is love ? And my heart said :
Desire of things unborn or things long dead.

There is scarcely ever happiness in this love ; at best, the luxury of remembering, which may not easily be distinguished from its torture. Self-centred, this lover feels that love is an abdication, a transfer of the key of one's inmost citadel, and into what insecure keeping !

Toujours ce compagnon dont le cœur n'est pas sur.

Love is the enemy, the troubler of the peace to which one may have attained as a materialist or as a dweller in one's ivory tower.

38

Modern Love

O that a man might live his life for a little tide
Without this rage in his heart, and without this foe at
    his side !
He could eat and sleep and be merry and forget, he could
    live well enough
Were it not for this thing that remembers and hates, and
    that hurts and is love.

Love is a glory, certainly, but it is incidentally
a humiliation from the masculine point of view,
an upsetting of values about which one may laugh
one's self into philosophy, but which, all the same,
will now and then seem intolerable.

> O why is it that a curl
> Or the eyelash of a girl,
> Or a glove she used to wear,
> Weighed with all a man has done,
> With a thought or with a throne,
> Drops the balance like a stone ?

For the question will arise more seriously, and it
will be an other than humorous mortification to
reflect that

> Yet as well can Kate or Nan
> Find, as Cleopatra can,
> Antony in any man.

" The modern malady of love," this poet declares, " is nerves " ; but it is something more. The trouble begins in what, being the most animal part of love, should be the most natural and happy, the desire of the body. But some of us moderns have educated the rut of the human animal, refined, complicated, exasperated it, until it is incapable of frank satisfaction, and demands, among other paradoxical things, in physical beauty the very reverse of that which promises satisfaction. The most sexual artist of Mr. Symons's generation, Aubrey Beardsley, produced in his expression of sensuality figures of which Mr. Symons has written :

" They have nothing of what is ' healthy ' or merely ' animal ' in their downward course towards repentance ; no overwhelming passion hurries them beyond themselves ; they do not capitulate to an open assault of the enemy of souls. It is the soul in them that sins, sorrowfully, without reluctance, inevitably. Their bodies are faint and eager with wantonness ; they desire more pleasure than there is in the world, fiercer and more exquisite pains, a more intolerable suspense. They have put off the common burdens of humanity, and put on that loneliness which is the rest of the saints and the unrest of those who have sinned with the intellect."

Well, a generation which had its suggestions of

feminine beauty from Rossetti, from Simeon
Solomon's half-realised dreams of figures that
almost equally symbolise sanctity and lust, from
Leonardo recovered, and delicately distorted, in
Pater's prose, or in literature from Rossetti again,
from the early Swinburne, from Baudelaire, and
found its typical artist in Aubrey Beardsley, was
incapable, so far as it had really responded to those
suggestions of mysticism, ambiguity, and perversity,
of content in simple possession. And, then, this
poet did not even desire content.

> *I have not loved love, nor sought happiness,*
> *I have loved every passionate distress,*
> *And the adoration of sharp fear and hate*
> *For love's sake, and what agonies await*
> *The unassuaged fulfilment of desire*
> *Not eased in the having ; I have sought to tire*
> *The fretting of the flesh grown sad with thought,*
> *And restless with remembering. . . .*

Amoris Victima he entitled the first volume in
which passion, with all its implications, became his
subject. In those poems, written in 1895–1896,
and in "Divisions on a Ground," 1897–1898,
"An Epilogue to Love," 1900–1904, and a few
single pieces in the volumes entitled *The Fool of
the World* and *Knave of Hearts*, we have some of the

41

subtlest dissections of love, as it is felt by a modern, very sensitive, very self-centred nature, that have ever been written. These poems, bound together, would take their place with Benjamin Constant's "Adolphe," the treatise of Stendhal, the poems of Donne, of Patmore, and how few other books of prose and verse, among the authorities on the subject. We pride ourselves on our psychological curiosity, our appreciation of psychological litera-ture, and we allow these extraordinary, painful, minutely truthful poems by Mr. Symons to be lost in the mass of his verse, and suppose him to be merely the poet of alcoves.

But my concern is with the poetry, as such, and I wish to draw attention, first of all, to the almost incredible lucidity of all this work. You could hardly have a more difficult subject ; it is in part Donne's, Meredith's ; but put these poems besides most of Donne's, or almost any of the pieces in "Modern Love," and you will be astonished by the limpidity of the writing. Here, if you like, is proof that verse is simpler than prose. It is from Browning, no doubt, that Mr. Symons had the hint to make verse vocal, but it is only the best part of the lesson that he has learned. There are no contortions, few parentheses and those the most natural, no breaks in the music, no lapses into the deplorably conversational. Only, the voice in

42

most of these poems is a recognisably human voice,
and it speaks from the heart, or from the troubled
nerves, with the most natural modulations and
pauses.

> *I only know I want you, only you,*
> *Only because I want you.   If you knew*
> *How much I want you ! If you knew how much*
> *I hunger, should I hunger, for your touch ?*

Could verse speak more directly, naturally, without
loss of music or poetic decorum ? And, except
for a passage in the final section of the *Amoris
Victima* volume, where rhetoric comes in with
conventional substance, could verse be more consistently kept on the level of the voice with which
a man tells his secrets ? There is in the writing
little of what would immediately and generally
be recognised as beauty. Here and there, but
probably not till a second reading, there may be
detected and detached a phrase or epithet separately
admirable, and we may suppose one reader in ten
disengaging from the context, for its imaginative
truth, a line or two in this poem or that :

> *I knew that death*
> *Which love is, ere it is eternity.*

But there is really no separable decoration in
these poems. Their style, to use such a word as

Mr. Symons would himself employ, is "lean"; their texture is closely woven; and even the most readily to be felt part of their beauty, the beauty of rhythm, is not so much in couplets or short passages as in the modulations of the voice, the delicate and natural distribution of emphasis, the flow and pause and return on itself of each confession as a whole.

They suffer, inevitably, from the old confusion between subject and expression, and because they deal so much with love as a malady or an insanity are presumed to be themselves dissolved in sick luxury or infirm in æsthetic purpose. But, actually, there is in them a clear-sighted and resolute aim, with an exceptional economy and lucidity in the use of words, and at times a tensity which hardly anyone in our time has rivalled. Let us not deceive ourselves. A poet might undertake to put love in its place as after all not quite the whole of life, might aspire to a more philosophical or more nobly enduring attitude towards it, and yet not give us one-tenth part of the evidence we have here of the poet's mastery of himself and of his art. The tension on these delicate lines is enormous, though it is never betrayed by the snapping of one thread in all this cobweb spun with a suicidal energy.

There are other poems of modern love by Mr.

44

Symons which claim attention—less the poems of a situation and therefore to be dealt with separately. In one or two of these the influence is less Donne, with whom he has a certain affinity, but with many differences, and whom he has really echoed only once, in writing in an early poem,

> *For God's sake let me love you, and give over*
> *These tedious protestations of a lover,*

or Browning, from whom he took no more than a hint, than Coventry Patmore. In very early manhood Mr. Symons, for a year or two, was much in the company of that strange, narrow, eagle-spirited man of genius, and he has written two acute and sympathetic criticisms of his work, but his own obligations to Patmore, curiously enough, have revealed themselves only rather late in life. They amount to little more than the loan, the adaptation, in a way the bettering, of a method of varying the length of the line in a form not unlike that of some of Patmore's Odes. Perhaps the most beautiful instance of his originality in something superficially like imitation is " The Ecstacy," from the group of poems entitled " The Loom of Dreams," produced between the dates of *Images of Good and Evil* and *The Fool of the World.*

Cease not, O never more
Cease,
To lift my joy, as upon windy wings,
Into that infinite ascension, where
In baths of glittering air,
It finds a heaven and like an angel sings.
Heaven waits above,
There where the clouds and fastnesses of love
Lift earth into the skies ;
And I have seen the glimmer of the gates,
And twice or thrice
Climbed half the difficult way,
Only to say
Heaven waits,
Only to fall away from paradise. . . .

The emotion of " reverence in extreme delight "
to which this poem is devoted, and which came to
this poet late and with all the value of surprise, is
in other poems written about 1900 and later.   It is
present in that poem " Love in Action," which, with
the exception of Donne's beautiful, extravagant,
and notorious " elegy," is the most audacious poem
of love in the language, and which has all the tact
in which Donne was deficient.   Think what is
said in this poem, without possibility of offence,
with the purity of passion, with only the transparent
and sufficing veil of art between us and the final
intimacies !

46

A mighty adoration came
Out of a smile to be a flame,
And the first breathings of desire
Were quickly blown into a fire
That took on both our bodies such
An intimate hold it seemed to touch
The soul of either to the quick,
And christen our vows catholic.
Then the beginning being over,
There was no more but love and lover.
And of that eternal minute
Know but that life and death were in it.
Only that being passed, I seem
Half to remember from a dream
Her panting breath across my eyes
And the whole amorous breast of sighs,
Her damp cheek and abandoned hair,
And mouth relaxed to that despair
Which is the shipwreck of each sense
In overflooding indolence ;
And in no dream, but even as one
Who wakes out of oblivion,
The quieting of aching throes,
Into a rapture of repose,
When eyes re-open and lips close.

The poet of *London Nights*, of love as a sensation, not the least frail and fleeting, and to be enjoyed with a fastidious greediness of which he is by no means the slave, has discovered not only the authentic agonies of love, but reverence. For the body of woman, first of all :

> *Wounded for our transgression, she must bear*
> *The crucifying, and the twelve-thorned crown*
> *And lay her secret pride shamefully down,*
> *That man may live, who is her lord and heir,*
> *Son of her travail, father of her pains,*
> *For his delight a bleeding sacrifice . . .*

> *Woman, when in the sacrament I take*
> *The bread, your body, and the wine, your kiss,*
> *I bid my body and soul remember this.*

There is no break with the past. This poet, as I have already insisted, is peculiarly the poet of memory, and he has stored up memories carefully with a luxurious anticipation of what their revival will mean. Perversity, ambiguity, the lure of artificial beauty will continue to appeal to his imagination, and there will never be any lack of stimulus to memory, sights, and sounds, and, especially, perfumes evocative of old days.

> *Peau d'Espagne, scent of sex, that brings*
> *To mind those ways wherein I went,*
> *Perhaps I might forget these things*
> *But for that infamy, your scent !*

Nothing of the past is lost. This poet includes, while he surpasses, the author of *Silhouettes* and *London Nights*. But he has come, after very ample experience, whether imaginary or other, of the sophistries and cruelties of love and of the artificial and perverse elements in the beauty of modern women, to a realisation of what is most natural and innocent and permanent in love and of the pathos in the mere fact of womanhood. If you like, he has arrived at the frontiers of commonplace. But in art the value of every discovery depends solely on the discoverer. The truth may be one of which all other men have long been in possession, but if the discoverer really has discovered it, for himself, with the surprise and illumination proper to discovery, it will have for him all the value of the most novel truth. And if he has the sincerity and the technique to convey it to us exactly as it struck him, silent upon a peak in Darien to which the trippers have crowded these many previous years, it will have no less a value for us. So in this originally and even now not very human poet there is a curious implicit pathos when he discovers that love can include friendship, can banish loneliness, can remove all reasons for the anxiety with which a spiritually solitary man flings himself into the crowds of cities and the general exterior movement of the world.

E

Arthur Symons

I loved the streets because
I feared myself and sought
In the crowd's hurry a pause
And sanctuary from thought.

My sanctuary is such
Now that I dwell with love
I cannot have too much
Of self or thought enough.

The poet of a certain agitating kind of modern love has become, at moments, the poet of love in its eternal aspects and qualities, and, as in " The Shadow," can say something essential about it with this finality :

When I am walking sadly or triumphantly,
With eyes that brood upon the smouldering thought
*   of you,*
And long desire and brief delight leap up anew,
Why is it that the eyes of all men turn to me ?
There's pity in the eyes of women as they turn,
And in the eyes of men self-pity, fear, desire :
As those who see the far-off shadow of a fire
Gaze earnestly, and wonder if their rooftrees burn.

He is still self-regarding, too much so to be a writer broadly and warmly human.

Modern Love

The world is a pulsation of my heart,
In me the beauty of the world exists.

And as we have just seen, the peace and liberty
love bring this poet finally do but enable him to say :

I cannot have too much
Of self or thought enough.

A certain aloofness from humanity remains.
Love, reconciling him to himself, cannot bring him
into any close relation with mankind. There remains, too, a certain coldness, as it may seem, of
temperament. His is a nature that does not kindle
easily or find any vehement joy in the liberty of the
flames, but it is retentive of heat, an exceptional
sensual memory aids it, and the embers are assur-
ance enough of conflagration though flames and
smoke have died away long before the poem begins
to be written.

IV

AMENDS TO NATURE

OUT of Baudelaire, no doubt, came that revolt against nature, taken whole and slavishly, which the wit of Whistler and of Wilde championed in England. Whistler's paradoxes were but the extravagances of an artist with an essentially just claim to establish; but Wilde's, often so delightful, sometimes so salutary at the moment of their utterance, betray now and then a confusion of what is natural with what is accidental; and I doubt whether many of the men of the 'nineties who professed an adoration of the artificial were quite clear about their æsthetics or quite sincere. We need not, at any rate, put Mr. Symons among them. He cared from the first for the artificial for reasons more worthy of considerations than those they improvised. He was not concerned to praise art as man's spirited reply to nature, to pit the artificial against the natural.

"Patchouli! Well, why not Patchouli?" he wrote in defence of his second volume of verse, "Is there any 'reason in nature' why we should write exclusively about the natural blush if the delicately acquired blush of rouge has any attraction for us ? Both exist : both, I think, are charming in their way : and the latter, as a subject, has, at all events, more novelty. If you prefer your ' new-mown hay ' in the hay-field, and I, it may be, in a scent-bottle, why may not my individual caprice be allowed to find expression as well as yours ? Probably I enjoy the hay-field as much as you do : but I enjoy quite other scents and sensations as well, and I take the former for granted, and write my poem, for a change, about the latter. I am always charmed to read beautiful poems about nature in the country. Only, personally, I prefer town to country, and in the town we have to find for ourselves, as best we may, the *décor* which is the town equivalent of the great natural *décor* of fields and hills. Here it is that artificiality comes in : and if anyone sees no beauty in the effects of arti-ficial light, in all the variable, most human, and yet most factitious town landscape, I can only pity him, and go on my own way."

The plea is only that the artificial—rouge, scent from the perfumers, the ballet, urban interiors, faces in a crowd revealed under unnatural light, the human comedy in full costume and with grease-paint duly applied—shall be admitted as a subject for poetry. The artificial is not preferred to the natural on any philosophical ground which we are called upon to accept. The preference is admittedly personal, and it is exercised in writing chiefly in the interests of novelty.

As a matter of fact, Mr. Symons even in those days, and even in the very volume he found it necessary to defend, showed on occasion a sensitive appreciation of natural colour and movement. It contained half a dozen poems on the scenery about Dieppe, where nature, it is true, was kept in her place by the presence, when Mr. Symons next returned to Dieppe, of Aubrey Beardsley. *London Nights* had a section entitled " Intermezzo : Pastoral," as well as more " colour studies " done at Dieppe. To be sure, Dieppe was not exactly a lodge in a vast wilderness, and only the *petits chevaux* careered over its prairies. But the meadow-grass at Mantua was allowed in one of the poems of this period to rebuke the sophistication of London :

> *But to have lain and loved the sun,*
> *Under the shadows of the trees,*
> *To have been found in unison,*
> *Once only, with the blessed sun ;*
>
> *Ah, in these flaring London nights,*
> *Where midnight withers into morn,*
> *How blissful a rebuke it writes*
> *Across the sky of London nights !*

54

Though an infrequent, Mr. Symons was not an unappreciative worshipper at the overcrowded shrine of nature. He never, at any rate, said to or about natural growths anything as rude as Baudelaire's " des légumes sanctifiés." But his appreciation then and for some years to come was that which he defined in a late poem of regret :

I have loved colours and not flowers ;
Their motion, not the swallow's wings ;
And wasted more than half my mortal hours
Without the comradeship of things.

We need not join in his mourning. Even poets are a little too apt to accept nature without discovering her. After that return to nature at the end of the eighteenth century the novelty, and perhaps the importance, of which used to be exaggerated till the other day, and may still be exaggerated by those who forget what Dyer did in " Grongar Hill " as far back as 1726, the subject is the most obvious that presents itself to an English poet. And to the Wordsworthian example had been added, in or before the years when Mr. Symons was beginning to read poetry, that of Tennyson, mere accuracy and abundance of natural detail, in which Tennyson, however, was sometimes surpassed by Lord de Tabley, being made in some quarters almost the

55

teſt of poetical excellence.   It was not altogether
a bad thing that Mr. Symons, as a rule, averted his
face from this recognised, this generally favoured
subjeƈt.   It ensured, at leaſt, a fine sincerity in his
eventual, half-reluƈtant discovery of it.

But in early days there was in his attitude towards
nature, as towards love, a kind of arrogance.   He
would ignore the organic relations of things and
disengage from them, for his private pleasure,
this or that quality which happened to appeal to
him :

> *Colours, and not flowers ;*
> *Their motion, not the swallow's wings.*

With the belated discovery that colour and movement muſt lose some of their significance when
abſtraƈted from the life to which they belong,
there awoke in him a new and touching humility.
As he has said, in a series of five poems dated 1907,
till then he had

> *walked as one*
> *Who dreams himself the maſter of the sun,*
> *And that the seasons are as seraphim*
> *And in the months and ſtars bow down to him.*

With the realisation that nature does not exiſt
simply as *décor* for the eyes of the individual, that

56

Pantarbo.

Salvator Rosa piled these rocks,
  Thus wildly under that wild light,
Or else fantastic Nature mocks
  His finite with her infinite

Grey ruinous heights that rise in towers,
  That fall in gorges down the steep,
Stark trees that never feel the showers,
  And rocky torrents buried deep;

Tormented wrathful ghosts of hills,
  That bear the scars of ancient woes,
And chafe beneath the doom that fills
  Their hollows with a loathed repose.

                    Arthur Symons

FACSIMILE OF MS. OF A POEM BY ARTHUR SYMONS.

there is something living and desiring him beyond
the lonely mirror of his sight, that man is part of
nature, comes the desire to abdicate.

And I have been of all men loneliest,
And my chill soul has withered in my breast
With pride and no content and loneliness.
And I have said : To make our sorrow less
Is there not pity in the heart of flowers,
Or joy in wings of birds that might be ours ?
Is there a beast that lives, and will not move
Towards our poor love with a more lovely love ?
And might not our proud hopeless sorrow pass
If we became as humble as the grass ?
I will get down from my sick throne where I
Dreamed that the seasons of the earth and sky,
The leash of months and stars, were mine to lead,
And pray to be the brother of a weed.

This new spirit of humility is accompanied by a
new infrequent joy in feeling kinship with nature,
by a willingness to be at times absorbed into her
life. The burden of identity, which unthinking
people bear without knowing it, and which must
at moments be so heavy on all who think, had
before this begun to weigh on Mr. Symons. In a
poem, I think one of his finest shorter poems,
written in 1898 and included in *Images of Good and*

Evil, Mr. Symons expressed it with remarkable subtlety, concision, and lucidity :

> *If I could know but why this care*
> *Is mine and not the care of man. . . .*
> *Why, knowing not from whence I came,*
> *Nor why I seek I know not what,*
> *I bear this heavy, separate name,*
> *While winds and waters bear it not.*
> *And why the unlimited earth delights*
> *In life, not knowing breath from breath,*
> *While I, that count my days and nights,*
> *Fear thought in life, and life in death.*

It is the boast of man to have acquired reason, and it has made him an exile, separating him, to the extent to which he relies on it, from a world in which all other creatures live by instinct. He bridges the gap between him and them, sometimes, with a friendship that is mostly condescension, not doubting that his position is wholly superior ; but this poet, having really thought out what the situation of man is, having at length apprehended it in the true imaginative way, and touched at last, proffers his friendship tentatively and humbly to " the little lords of day and night." No longer does he look on the world " with usurping eyes " ; it is theirs, by the measure

58

of their nearness to nature, more than his. One
step more :

> *I feel, in every midge that hums,*
> *Life, fugitive and infinite,*
> *And suddenly the world becomes*
> *A part of me and I of it.*

He has arrived at the point at which he can
write :

> *What is it in the earth, the air,*
> *The smell of autumn, or the rare*
> *And half-reluctant harmonies*
> *The mist weaves out of silken skies,*
> *What is it that shuts my brain and brings*
> *These sleepy dim awakenings*
> *Till I and all things seem to be*
> *Kin and companion to a tree ?*

He finds his definite friendship in intimacy with
a dog. Where else should anyone find it ? The dog,
alone out of what brutes call the brute creation, has
real need of man, and, as I have written in another
context, the only quite indisputable argument for
the continuation of the human race is that a world
empty of men would be intolerable to dogs. But
this friendship of his, instead of being the ordinary
affair of easy sentiment with the creature's devotion

taken for granted, becomes suggestive to him and significant to us, because there is surprise, with a delicate pathos, in the discovery that what people in general take as a matter of course is possible, and for him.   The poems on this dog, *Api,* though two of them will deserve a place in any special anthology, are perhaps no great matter.   The affecting prose introduction to them is of real importance in an attempt to understand Mr. Symons. After the death of his friend he writes :

" For nearly a year I have been normal, human, like other people, no longer isolated from the men and women whom I met in the street, but with a new feeling of belonging to them by at least one link of friendliness.   The link has gone now, and I walk more lonely, in a self-absorption now wholly returned upon itself. . . .

" Sometimes I say to myself, How great a burden of love is taken off my heart !   The scales are even now ;   there is nothing to weigh down one or the other.   It is horrible to have one's heart in an even balance.   It is the average way of being happy. . . .

" Is there reason why one's love for a dog is so like what one's love may be for a woman, that they are so near a part of the earth, and so have a kind of wonder for us, and a desire for impossible possession? Both are in their way helpless and speechless, and touch us by what is unconscious in them, and a savour that does not seem to us, judging by ourselves, quite human."

The discovery that " there are beings to be pitied everywhere " in a world of which man has usurped the lordship, the discovery that nature in her totality can mean so much to man instead of being merely in her incidentals a delight to the connoisseur of forms and colours, lead this poet into no rhetorical exaggeration of the degree of intimacy attainable. Indeed, the new brotherliness towards animals (never towards man!) has hardly stirred in him, the sense of union with nature has barely awakened, when he becomes acutely aware of the isolation to which the human being is condemned, if no longer by pride, then by the ordering of the universe. The artist may propose to himself to write, in the words of Whitman, " with the perfect rectitude and insouciance of the movement of all animals," but to his gain and loss he can never arrive at quite that. He may seek to blend with nature, but even in the rare moments when he feels that he is becoming one with her, there will come the doubt whether she is more than a projection of his own dreams.

Arthur Symons

Yet there is beauty, real as a pain,
In this inconstant show of green and blue
That, like the unfelt air, I travel through,
Yet closes round me like the air again.
This carpet the smooth grass,
These azure hangings laced with silken white,
This leafy rustle, this bright watery stir,
All colours of the day and night,
That come, and are forgotten, and so pass,
Are they not each a delicate minister
And patient handmaid of delight ?
Shadows they are, and shadows that I make
They may be : what am I ?
I hear an echo and a voice reply :
A dreamer dreaming that he is awake.

Shadows or realities, of our own making or independent, there the great natural phenomena are, and we may at least refrain from reading our own fancies into them. In his " Hymn to the Sea," which has the lovely phrase about the sea-wind blowing from beyond " the mild and sweet half-human regions of the rose," Mr. Symons has his characteristic rebuke to those poets who would make the sea the mere mirror of their own moods, reducing the most sublime and inscrutable thing in nature to a private looking-glass. And in the " Hymn to Earth," from which I have just quoted, he rebukes himself out of the mouth of nature :

> *Think thou, as I, thy solitary thought ;*
> *Trouble me not.*

Is it the " comradeship of things " that he has become aware of, or the quality of his no longer contented loneliness ? He has found, at any rate, this once arrogant poet of the artificial, a subject which arouses in him an unexpected humility, and being still the man he was, he is half at a loss with it ; whence a tentativeness, a delicate ceremoniousness, a hesitancy in putting forth claims, curiously touching to those who can perceive the situation. His technique was never more, nor he himself less assured than in certain of these pondered, wistful amends to nature.

And he has other amends to make, on behalf of those

> *Thy creatures, that have wandered from that line*
> *Thou sett' st them out of chaos, that have gone*
> *About their many businesses, not Thine,*
> *Saying let my will, not Thy will be done;*
> *Idolatrous, deeming themselves divine,*
> *Bowing down each other to the other for a sign,*
> *Working for Thee in evil ways that run*
> *Quite round the circle of Thy pure design,*
> *Yet swerve not from the centre.*

63

Only to man he has no apology to offer. When Baudelaire received from Victor Hugo a volume with the inscription *Jungamus dextras,* he wrote to Madame Paul Meurice : " Je connais les dessous du Latin de Victor Hugo. Cela veut dire : unissons nos mains, *pour sauver le genre humain.* Mais je me fiche du genre humain." And Mr. Symons is unconcerned about humanity at large or in any of its subdivisions.* There is no hatred ; why should there be ? One must be Abel's brother to have Cain's feelings. Mr. Symons has never been conscious of the brotherhood of man. He declared to me once, over a dinner-table, that misunder-standing of him, of which it would never occur to him to complain, was due to the fact that he was Cornish ; but without doubting that Cornish blood, the strain to which wreckers and revivalists con-tributed, may have helped to remove him a step from English sympathy, I could but smile at the suggestion, if he was suggesting so much, that he could have been almost everyone's friend or almost everyone's poet among his own people. He would be, in a sense, a foreigner anywhere. In con-versation with one of whose sympathy and admira-tion he is sure, on subjects that matter profoundly to

* He has not written a single poem in expression of actual or imagined national emotion ; nor has he anywhere hymned the hypothetical general hopes of mankind.

him, he will sometimes, in the very act of agreement, look at his companion with alienation, with the eyes of one awakening out of a lonely dream to find it unaccountably shared by an intruder ; or he will pause, between one high-pitched sentence and another, with a smile in which a certain childish mischief mixes with a malicious confidence that there at least his companion does not follow him. His interest in the best part of one, in one's ideas, when one has any, in one's enthusiasm for a few things that matter supremely, is of the most delicate generosity, but he is totally devoid of that interest in the unessential part of one that friends feel. He cares for human beings in so far as they are, in the most liberal sense, artists ; he is surprised, touched, uneasy, when trapped into caring for them simply as human beings.

And so, in writing *Spiritual Adventures*, doubtless the best thing done, in anything like the spirit of Pater, since Pater's own " Imaginary Portraits," it is only portions of each character that he gives us. Indeed, he gives us hardly more than the æsthetic temperament of each. Impossible, one would say, that he should give us more. But this apparently impossible thing he has in fact done, in a poetic tragedy, the most important single achievement of his career, and to it I propose devoting nearly the whole of the next section of this book.

F

V

THE TRAGEDIES

ON the appearance of the first volume of verse published by Mr. Symons, George Meredith wrote to him acutely predicting that he would end by producing poetic drama. Never was fulfilled prophecy more nearly unfulfilled. For though Mr. Symons turned to drama very early, with a play which was produced in London at the beginning of the 'nineties but of which, if it ever existed in any form but the actors' scrip, no trace now remains, and though in maturity he continued to write dramatic studies or sketches, the years went by and drama, in the strict sense, remained unachieved. What we had from him were exercises in dramatic form, legitimate enough, graceful enough, but without the vitality of drama. The best of them were as far removed from the real thing as moralities and masques. " Mary in Bethlehem " was on its level a beautiful thing, with a most happy blending of innocency and art in certain of the speeches. " The Lover of the Queen of Sheba " was a charming thing, luxurious

66

and melancholy in that way which, after Swinburne and Christina Rossetti, almost any good
writer can travel when he sets out to tell a quasi-
Biblical tale. "The Fool of the World" was
genuinely impressive, and is among the most
significant things that the writer, haunted as he is
by the mystery of death, has ever done ; but, of
course, it used symbolical figures, not human
characters. The more definitely dramatic am-
bitions disclosed in some of the scenes Mr. Symons
wrote—" Otho and Poppæa " and " The Death of
Agrippina "—seemed destined to remain unrealised.
And—if it be a confession of stupidity, let it be made
candidly—the present critic, for one, was astonished
when, on the appearance of *Tragedies* in 1916,
he saw what Mr. Symons had done in " The
Harvesters."

Surprise would have been diminished if it had
been possible to read before it the play " Cleopatra
in Judæa," which, with " The Death of Agrippina,"
accompanied it. For " Cleopatra " is in its degree
drama. I was in India when it was acted in
London, and if there has been another opportunity of seeing it on the stage I have missed it ;
but in reading it I can well believe that it would
act, that the audience would feel real an increasing
suspense, and finally draw a breath of genuine relief.
But it is a dramatic situation rather than a drama

in the full sense, and thus hardly a preparation for
" The Harvesters."

That situation is made clear at the very beginning
of " Cleopatra in Judæa " by Herod's speech :

> Consider who she is
> Whom now I hold, whom now I hold or loose.
> She covets all Judæa, as a fog
> Sucks up the watery life-blood of the earth
> She has sucked up the cities of the plain
> From Egypt to Eleutherus, save Tyre
> And Sidon, both free cities.   Syria
> She has already, and Arabia
> She hopes for, and she comes from Antony
> Gone against Artabazes, to subdue
> Armenia, that he may give this woman
> A kingdom for a bracelet on her wrist . . .
> O Antony
> Has kissed away the world, and now the queen
> Sets politic bounds to appetite, and stints
> Her choicest lusts, lest, for a bankrupt love,
> He snatch at no more kingdoms.   Counsel me
> What shall I do with this wise enemy,
> Now my most perilous guest ?

Herod listens to various advice, but resolves to
make an end of Cleopatra. She comes to him,
uses her wiles on him, suggests to him cunningly

that Antony lusts after Mariamne, who will be safe
from Antony only so long as she, Cleopatra, lives.
When he has left her, and Iras hastens in to announce
a plot against her, Cleopatra can triumphantly
reply,

> *I have saved myself ; Mariamne, whom I hate,*
> *Has saved me, and I have not wholly failed.*

The firm development of a single situation, with
characters under the sway of the hour's motives, is
no guarantee of power to handle gradually evolving
action and characters in whom the whole range
of emotion must be felt, and " The Harvesters "
remains only a little less surprising after reading
" Cleopatra."

Shelley set " The Cenci " apart from all his other
work with the curious label, " a work of art."
Mr. Symons, I do not need to be reminded, is not
the equal of Shelley, and " The Harvesters " is not
on an equality with " The Cenci," but it is as
exceptional a thing in its author's work. It is
exceptional in two ways, in the creation of character,
so to speak, in the round instead of the presentation
of profiles, and in the self-denial and skill with which
the style has been subdued to the probabilities of
peasant speech. But, exceptional as it is, it is
everywhere very evidently its author's work,

69

thoroughly characteristic in its antinomianism, in the subtlety of its simplicity, in the delicate vocal quality of the verse.

The action of " The Harvesters " takes place at St. Ruan, a village in Cornwall, in the early part of the nineteenth century. In Act I we are in Michael Raven's cottage. Three women are at the table, drinking tea ; Mary Raven has just set the kettle back on the hearth. Vecchan, the village " innocent," is heard off, singing of birth and death. They talk of her, Mary upholding her, Jane Angrove frightened of her. By a natural transition, the talk turns to Mary herself : is her father, Michael Raven, aware of gossip about her and Peter Corin ? One of the women, Tamson Trembath, speaks to Mary in earnest, warning her of the danger of her conduct. Mary retorts, asking by what right people gossip of her and Peter Corin, and Ann Saundry, a widow, whose husband has been lost at sea, intervenes :

Don't heed them, Mary ; and let Tamson talk :
There's many things much worse to bear than talk,
You don't know what it is to sit and think,
And hear the wind, when you've a man at sea,
Nor when there's nothing left to think of.
MARY :   *No,*
I don't know that.

TAMSON :   *Ann's thinking all day long*
Of things that won't be mended ; there are things
Thinking might mend.
        ANN :   *They are not worth the thought.*
It's not the real things you think about,
But women's words, fancies of boys and men,
The good name of a maid or of a man.
The good name of a maid or of a man
Is neither life nor death.

Tamson's reply is that, if Mary will not heed her, she will have to heed her father, who must soon know of her relations with Peter Corin. The father enters. He has been to the chapel, and is asked if he saw any of the neighbours there, to which he answers that he went to seek not his neighbours but the Lord.

TAMSON :   *You are as bitter, Michael,*
As if you had not found Him . . .
                You'd not forgive
A neighbour's talk against you in his sleep.

All this preparatory matter, written with a sober skill, is quite admirable. No character has made what our general experience of modern poetical drama would lead us to call a speech, but already we know something of the essence of each character.

But immediately we are to know much more of
Mary, of Michael, and of Peter Corin. The women
gone, Michael questions his daughter, and then tells
her he will keep her and the illegitimate child that
is to be born, but will never speak to her again.
He leaves her, and Peter comes, to learn that she is
about to have a child by him, and thereupon to
reason with her, plausibly, basely, and to part from
her, bidding her " bide still and wait."

Act II is set in the harvest-field in August. The
women discuss Mary's position and the conduct
of her father : " that man," says Ann, " would be
as righteous as God is." It is Ann who best
understands Michael and Mary :

> *There are women who step in*
> *Knee-deep into the slough, and then step back*
> *A little fouled, and wash their feet of it,*
> *And go their way.   But she's not one of such.*
> *If Mary gave her heart to any man*
> *She would keep nothing over ; and for that,*
> *She is the cleaner and the honester,*
> *And liker to her father.   He and she,*
> *Father and daughter, have an equal will :*
> *His will not bend and hers can only break.*

Michael is asleep in the field, weary with sharpen-
ing scythes. Peter Corin is at work at the other

end of the field, and presently a boy brings Peter's sickle to be sharpened by the awakened Michael. Then Mary, nearing her time, approaches Michael, and speaks to him, but in vain. Vecchan has here a speech, with a certain grotesque effectiveness, but leaves us a little uncertain of the inevitability of her words. But now Peter Corin and Mary are face to face, and Mary, now knowing her lover to the bone, cuts down to it in her answer to his overtures :

> *My father casts me off ;*
> *You do not cast me off.   O no, your greed*
> *Clutches with all its fingers at the crumbs*
> *They scattered from the table.*

Yet she thinks his renewed protestations mean he is going to marry her. Then, grasping his real meaning, she kills him with his sickle, and Vecchan comes in, singing : " Put down the sickle, for all the harvest is in."

In Act III we are in the market-place of St. Ruan. Those present are waiting for the arrival of the coach, which will have amongst its passengers Mary Raven, for she has been pardoned and released, the law holding that she had extremest provocation and acted while beside herself. Her father is there ; with him the boy who in Act II took Corin's scythe to be sharpened. Effectively

73

enough, and plausibly, but perhaps a little too faithfully to the tradition established by Webster and
other dramatists, the boy, in his simple questioning,
probes the old man's wound.   The women of the
village talk of Mary—Ann, as ever, being the one
that understands and pities.   The coach arrives,
and the sightseers can gape, but a sailor in the crowd
turns away :

> *It's not for us to judge her, but to go*
> *Out of the sight and judgment of her eyes.*

Mary finds her father still will not speak to her,
and there follows a revealing dialogue between Mary
and Ann.

> MARY : *I have been blind, but justice is blind too,*
> *If this is justice that has come on me.*
> ANN : *The law was merciful.*
> MARY :   *The law ? I mean*
> *The justice that made women and made men.*
> ANN : *What sort of justice ?*
> MARY :   *That which gave a woman*
> *A body to be loved, and gave a man*
> *The power to love a woman, and then gave*
> *A man the power not to forget the woman*
> *But only to forget love.   Why, that justice.*
> ANN : *You have nothing to repent of ?*

MARY :   *All the past*
Was like a thing worn out and put away,
Not to be thought of any more ; I seemed
To drift with present time as with a tide,
And there was no beginning and no end.
And when I thought, and tried to stop the tide
By thinking, I was clutching at a weed
That the tide carried, and I hardly knew
If I were tide or seaweed or some dream
Of sea-birds gibbering at an ashen moon.

There is no penitence in Mary.   Rather does she
question all the conventional morality arrayed
against her.

Shall I not say
Father was wrong, father has done me wrong?
Has he not sold my happiness and his
For heavy empty syllables that weigh
False in the balances ? There's sin, a name,
Justice, a name, repentance, right and wrong,
Names ; he would hold them in his hand, and stand
Like a proud, ignorant child, clutching his toys,
In God's place, more inflexible than God.

And Vecchan calls her to live henceforth with
nature, and she passes out of the order and judgment of society, leaving Michael Raven to cry out,

Lord, Lord, if she were right, if she were right !

75

The play of which I have given this summary is not rich in the qualities we have been taught to expect in modern poetical drama. It has none of the wealth of magnificent poetry which Swinburne's plays offer us, none of the enchantment which many of the plays of Mr. Yeats offer us, and to some readers may seem rather bare and flat. Nor is it flawless, for Vecchan, who should speak with the voice of nature herself, has speeches that ring rather doubtfully. But it is work of an unexpected breadth and, within limits which are scarcely felt, of a still more unexpected humanity. It is, as writing, an extraordinary instance of the self-denial through which the true self of the poet is realised, his natural subtlety and delicacy coming through the simplicity. And it is drama expressed in poetry, not poetry with a dramatic excuse.

There is nothing else in the dramatic work of its author to set beside it. *Tristan and Iseult*, announced many years earlier as in preparation and published a year later, with a dedication to Eleanora Duse, has a great theme, concentration, dignity, with some scenes effective in the good sense, not written for effect. But it never burns with the passion that is required by the subject. *The Toy Cart*, a play in four acts, in prose, founded on the " Mrichhakati " of Sudaraka, is hardly more than a literary exercise. We are left, then, with *The*

Harvesters as evidence that Mr. Symons, the most subjective of poets, can write vital drama on the grand scale.

The Harvesters is a masterpiece, but of a kind that appearing even early in its author's career would not have excited hope of ample, fully vitalised dramatic production. Except for something dubious in the speeches of the girl who is God's fool, Vecchan, it realises everywhere what we may suppose to have been its writer's intentions, but there is a kind of spareness in it. It does not suggest the economy of a dramatist curbing his prodigality, but that of one who, visited by a rare inspiration, has carefully proved himself adequate. Yet how fine a play it is, how genuinely and surprisingly human within its limits, how truly tragic, how exquisitely tactful in the subdual of the style !

VI

THE STUDIES IN LITERATURE

TO its inestimable advantage, the criticism of Mr. Symons has always been a poet's; to its considerable risk, it has always been that of a poet whose creative power is not exhausted in his poetry. At its best, it gives us the truth about a writer's work as we have that work, a discreetly generous expansion of the work to the full measure of its author's intention, and a suggestion of the value of the work in the critic's own imaginative world. We pause, then, between essay and essay with the feeling that we have been put in possession of the *vraie vérité* about the work, the worker's whole ambition, the critic. We think over the essay again, reflecting that the triple revelation has been given us without sign of effort on the critic's part, infallibly, inevitably, to the murmur of a prose that flows carefully indeed, since it is conveying something more intimate and precious than mere opinion, but as naturally as the recital of a man's most sacred

78

experiences to the one possible confidant. There has been no design on us, there has been no attempt to exploit the writer under consideration in the interests of a private scheme of æsthetics. Simply, in doing justice, sensitively and imaginatively, to a writer, this critic has won us, and placed the writer not only in literature, but in the critic's own world. It is impossible to be too grateful for such criticism, and there is page after page of it in *The Symbolist Movement in Literature, Studies in Prose and Verse, The Romantic Movement in English Poetry.*

But Mr. Symons, partly, we may assume, through natural limitations, partly through concentration on the task of dissecting his own moods, has found in writing his poetry something less than the complete satisfaction of his creative impulses. As a critic, therefore, he has on occasion been tempted, very likely without being aware of it, to write a not quite legitimately creative criticism. Never, or scarcely ever, in dealing with literature ! The intellectual content of literature discourages anything of the kind. Pictures, music, buildings, cities are quite another matter. You cannot quote them as you may quote prose and verse ; you must in some sort reproduce them in terms of literature in criticising them ; you must translate them.

Now Mr. Symons is comparable with Shelley,

79

Frere, FitzGerald and Rossetti as a translator of poetry into poetry, more accurate than the first could or the third cared to be, and as sensitive as the last. Several of his versions from Verlaine are miracles; he has done not less miraculously in the only versions he has made from Mallarmé; and, to say nothing of other successes in verse, there are some of the prose renderings of Baudelaire's " Petits Poèmes en Prose," almost incredibly faithful to the rhythms as well as the substance of the original. But no one has yet found out how to translate pictures and music into words with the same conviction. Lamb, in a magnificent sentence, reproduces a Titian; Swinburne, in an anticipation of Pater's method though in a very different manner, gives us a drawing by Leonardo; Pater has his celebrated successes; there are some extraordinary triumphs by Mr. D. S. MacColl; there are some by Mr. Symons himself; and, looking about diligently, one could find other instances. They prove only that genius can intermittently do the impossible. For the most part, and even in Pater, the reproduction is a private version, suggestive, valuable, too, for what it tells us of the critic, but not indisputably the equivalent of what was on the canvas.

It is, then, in their inevitability that the essays in which Mr. Symons has dealt with literature are superior, in the mass, to those in which he has dealt with the other arts.

The most evident merit of his literary criticism, when we view it as a whole, is its catholicity. St. Augustine, to an edition of whose Confessions he prefixed one of the most acutely appreciative essays ever written on the subject, or Casanova, in whose archives he made important discoveries at Dux; Christina Rossetti or Baudelaire; an Elizabethan dramatist or Ibsen: he exposes himself to each with the same receptivity, deals with each with the same scrupulous care. Caring so much for what is most essentially artistic in art, he might have come to value too highly those writers in whom the love of beauty is most conscious of itself, but who are in achievement minors. Caring so much for what is strange in life, he might have given too much of his attention to the curiosities and the morbidities of beauty. But he is nowhere to be found forgetting that the main way of literature is after all the main way, or that style at its highest may be found in a master writing out of a careless prodigality as well as in the devotees of the *mot juste*. I am not at all sure that he has not, on the whole, written even more penetratingly of authors outside what might be expected to be his most intimate circle than of those who are akin to him, the challenge bringing all his critical intelligence

G

into an even more than usually patient and resolute
endeavour to reach the inner truth. There are,
indeed, writers whom he has passed by in silence,
and notably the English novelists. But there are
few names of the first or second order in the literatures of England and France which are not in the
contents lists of his volumes of criticism or have had
from him less than justice. Cumulatively, without
extravagance about any one of them, he may slightly
have overpraised both the Elizabethan dramatists
and the modern French Symbolist writers ; but
he has never been the dupe of bad work coming to
him with prestige or with irrelevant attractions,
and again and again he has elicited from writers
whom we thought we knew completely some charm
or power to which we can never again be insensible,
but which we had hardly so much as suspected.

Turn the pages of Mr. Symons's prose, and you
will come at every other moment, not on epigrams,
but on phrases and sentences which sum up the
finer truth about a writer as if it had concentrated
itself there without effort on his part. When he
says of Balzac that he is the equivalent of great
cities ; of Keats that he had only the point of view
of the sunlight ; of Merimée that he combined the
curiosity of the student with the indifference of the
man of the world, and that his stories are " detached
as it were from their own sentiments " ; of Gautier

82

that he had no secrets of his own, and could keep none of nature's ; of Lamb's that his is in the finer sense " mortal wit " ; and when, in a casual turning of the pages, you find scores of such things, you know that the critic is one who has penetrated to the core of his subjects. Look a little more carefully, and you will come upon instances of that rarest expression of critical truth in which the soul of a book or a writer is incarnated in some exact, beautiful image, comparable with the most famous in Coleridge, in Lamb. And there is something else, never, I think, so far recognised with any cordiality, to reward the reader who is looking for incidental excellences instead of at the work as a whole : a delicate, cultivated, seldom exercised but damaging wit. There are a good many examples of it in the briefest notices in *The Romantic Movement in English Poetry*, and you may find it elsewhere, but I will illustrate it by a sentence from an article on Francis Thompson : " But the feast he spreads for us is a very Trimalchio's feast, the heaped profusion, the vaunting prodigality, which brings a surfeit ; and, unlike Trimalchio, it could not be said of him, *Omnia domi nascuntur*." If a thing so good had been said by the late Mr. Andrew Lang or by Mr. Birrell, by any of our recognised literary wits, it would have gone the round of the town.

Arthur Symons

But it would be rather trivial to insist further on the felicity of single judgments in the work of a critic with such aims as Mr. Symons's. We have to consider his literary criticism in its cumulative effect in certain departments, and then what as a whole it tells of literature and of the critic himself.

His first volume of critical essays, the *Studies in Two Literatures*, has disappeared, portions of its contents reappearing in the *Studies in Prose and Verse*, portions in *Studies in Elizabethan Drama*. The title has been revived, in the collected edition of his Works, to cover a very unfortunately composed book into which *The Symbolist Movement in Literature* has been absorbed. If there was one volume of his criticism which deserved to have its integrity respected it was *The Symbolist Movement*, the least miscellaneous of all its author's critical work.

One thing only can be urged against that book. It was written with a kind of millennial expectation, at a date when Symbolism, like Alfred de Musset in Heine's epigram, had its future behind it. Symbolism, as it exists in the work of Gérard de Nerval, to whom, under his insane or illuminated aspect, Mr. Symons rightly and clearly traced it, in the work of Villiers de l'Isle-Adam, Rimbaud, Laforgue, Mallarmé, and, more doubtfully, in that of Verlaine, is a liberation from the pressure of material-

84

ism, and of that kind of literature which deals with exterior appearances and would " build with bricks and mortar within the covers of a book." But no sooner is man free from one kind of captivity than he organises another. Symbolism was not in fact the establishment of a new, enduring freedom for literature, but the disintegration of the old tyranny in preparation for an anarchy which still endures and the tyrannies of which, though petty and individually avoidable, are in the aggregate not less oppressive. Literature is inevitably a compromise, and, however much a particular man of genius may gain by neglecting the claim of one part of its substance, general progress by indefinitely increased neglect of that part is impossible. So when Mr. Symons tells us : " here, then, in this revolt against exteriority, against a materialistic tradition ; in this endeavour to disengage the ultimate essence, the soul, of whatever exists and can be realised by the consciousness ; in this dutiful waiting upon every symbol by which the soul of things can be made visible ; literature, bowed down by so many burdens, may at last attain liberty, and its authentic speech," we feel he is announcing something which not only has not come to pass, but never could.

Mr. Symons, it is plain, expected too much of Symbolism as a movement, as a general literary influence. It is not characteristic of him to fall, even momentarily, into the errors of those who attach much importance to movements. He knows well enough, and indeed no one has said it more sharply, that there are no new truths in art, only old truths which from time to time it becomes necessary to rediscover. As, in writing of the romantic poetry produced in England in the first quarter of the nineteenth century, he rightly insisted that, except in a more conscious and in the best sense economical use of imagination, it was at one with the genuine poetry of every other age in this country, so in writing of the Symbolists he was careful to remind us that " Symbolism, as seen in the writers of our day, would have no value if it were not seen also, under one disguise or another, in every great imaginative writer." It was not the novelty of Symbolism or its value, but the chances of its indefinite development, that he exaggerated.

Yet with the Symbolist writers themselves he dealt with a remarkable discretion, keeping his balance in the treatment of those who were most unbalanced. Gérard de Nerval has long had friends in England, but so far as I am aware no one here really suspected what was implied in the stranger part of his work, the lovely and mysterious sonnets, and " Le Rêve et la Vie," until Mr. Symons published his essay. Villiers, again, though it is impossible that any intelligent reader can have failed to recognise his gifts as a teller of tales and as a master of spiritual irony, had never been made to yield up his philosophy to us till Mr. Symons wrote. In dealing with Rimbaud and with Jules Laforgue, Mr. Symons had been preceded by Mr. George Moore ; but has anyone, even in France, where there is ampler criticism of these two writers, said anything so fundamental about them ?

Take this, about the central mystery of the wonderful, and, I will add, detestable boy who created a new poetry, and then forsook literature to traffic in gold and ivory in Africa :

" 'The secret of Rimbaud, I think, and the reason he was able to do the unique thing in literature which he did, and then to disappear quietly and become a legend in the East, is that his mind was not the mind of the artist, but of the man of action. He was a dreamer, but all his dreams were discoveries. To him it was an identical act of the temperament to write the sonnets of the Vowels, and to trade in ivory and frankincense with the Arabs. He lived with all his faculties at every instant of his life, abandoning himself to himself with a confidence which was at once his strength and (looking at things less absolutely) his weakness. To the student of success, and what is relative in achievement, he illustrates the danger of one's over-possession by one's own genius, just as aptly as the saint in the cloister does, or the mystic too full of God to speak intelligibly to the world, or the spilt wisdom of the drunkard. . . . But there are certain natures (great or small, Shakespeare or Rimbaud, it makes no difference) to whom the work is nothing, the act of working everything. Rimbaud was a small, narrow, hard, precipitate nature, which had the will to live, and nothing but the will to live ; and his verses, and his follies, and his wanderings, and his traffickings were but the breathing of different hours in his day."

But the central figure in that book on *The Symbolist Movement in Literature,* and after Pater the chief influence on Mr. Symons as a theorist, was Mallarmé. It is no doubt inadequate to say that Mallarmé was in revolt, in his aloof and gentle way, against this or that in the literature of the generation preceding his own ; he was in revolt, in a sense, against the nature of literature, against all that tethers it to the earth, giving it, however, its greatest opportunities in the compromise it makes at the expense of part of its freedom. Consider some of the ideas of Mallarmé :

" Poetry is the language of a state of crisis."
" Symbolist, Decadent, or Mystic, the schools thus called by themselves, or thus hastily labelled

88

by our information-press, adopt, for meeting-place, the point of an Idealism which (in the same way as in fugues, in sonatas) rejects the ' natural ' materials, and, as brutal, a direct thought ordering them, to retain no more than a suggestion.   To be instituted, a relation between images—exact, and that therefrom should detach itself a third aspect, fusible and clear, offered to the divination.   Abolished the pretension, æsthetically an error, despite its dominion over almost all the masterpieces, to enclose within the subtle paper other than, for example, the horror of the forest, or the silent thunder afloat in the leaves, not the intrinsic, dense wood of the trees. . . ."

" The pure work implies the elocutionary disappearance of the poet, who yields to the words, immobilised by the shock of their inequality ; they take light from mutual reflections, like an actual trail of fire over precious stones, replacing the old lyric efflatus or the enthusiastic personal direction of the phrase."

There, certainly, is what all the Symbolists aimed at, only not so consciously and uncompromisingly as Mallarmé.   And this aim has also, with as a rule very much less consciousness of it, and under many disguises, been intermittently the aim of most of the greatest poets of the past, their instinct saving them from a too determined and sterilising devotion to it.   Evocation, not description, though it may be in the midst of a complacent enough attempt at description ; the suggestion of the secret links between things ; the mysterious kindling of fire from one word to another ; the instilling into the mind of the reader of an energy which shall oblige him to complete pictures which the greatest of poets must leave only half painted : all that is common to the genuine poetry of every age and school. It is not so much in the character of the architecture as in the denial of a glimpse of the plan that Mallarmé differs from the poets of the past. But his contempt for fact, for all that part of poetry of which Verlaine scornfully said, " all the rest is literature," was the more emphatic because he came just after an age in which, in France, fact had been over-valued.

Mr. Symons has had his own contemptuous word to say of fact in literature, in the Introduction to his *Studies in Prose and Verse* :

" Unfortunately, words can convey facts ; unfortunately, people in general have an ill-regulated but insatiable appetite for facts. Now music cannot convey facts at all ; painting or sculpture can only convey fact through a medium, which necessarily transforms it. But literature is tied by that which gives it wings. It can do, in a measure, all that can be done by the other arts, and it can speak where they can but make beautiful and expressive

ISLAND COTTAGE, WITTERSHAM, KENT, THE COUNTRY
HOME OF ARTHUR SYMONS.

gestures. But it has this danger, that its paint, or clay or crotchets and quavers, may be taken from the colour, or form, or sound, and not as the ministrants of these things. Literature, in making its beautiful piece of work, has to make use of words and facts ; these words, these facts, are the common property of all the world, to whom they mean no more than what each individually says, before it has come to take on beautiful form through its adjustment in the pattern."

Mr. Symons sees the danger peculiar to literature, but he is not driven by his perception of it to rejection of the compromise by which literature exists as more than a small collection of exceptional, remote, shadowy masterpieces, of the tribe of " Kubla Khan." No English critic has insisted more on the necessity of the transformation of fact, but insistence on transformation is one thing, rejection of every kind of fact which cannot be so trans-formed as to lose all trace of earthly origin is another. The applause we give to the alchemist, after all, is for showing us as gold that which was base metal. If it is simply the sight of gold that will set us applauding, we need go no farther than the mint. Well, the tendency of those who, by temperament or theory, take the central doctrines of Symbolism too literally is to work only on gold, or on what will most readily transmute into it,

91

and Mr. Symons, in writing with a most generous
sympathy about Villiers de l'Isle-Adam, is con-
strained to rebuke him gently for his exclusive pre-
occupation with the most exalted and exceptional
characters : " But he does not realise, as the great
novelists have realised, that stupidity can be
pathetic, and that there is not a peasant, nor even
a self-satisfied bourgeois, in whom the soul has not
its part, in whose existence it is not possible to be
interested."

Mr. Symons, indeed, has never shown more
clearly than in the careful reservations in *The
Symbolist Movement in Literature,* where he was
dealing with writers who peculiarly engage his
sympathy, the unwavering æsthetic common-sense
underlying his responsiveness to the subtlest and
strangest form of beauty. It is with a certain effect
of anti-climax that one mentions that modest but
not too common merit. Yet is it not, when found
in a subtle, curious, hypersensitive artist, worthy
to be dwelt upon ? A great part of the seemingly
arrogant self-defence which Whistler conducted,
with paradoxical wit, for so many years was directed,
and not unnecessarily, towards establishing the
truth that he knew the alphabet of his art, and had
its common-sense. And, in dealing with a critic
who has shown, at times, a preference for difficult
cases, who has followed the modern imagination

on some of its most secret and dangerous journeys, and who has sometimes called upon us, rightly, to hear the hymn to beauty where it is sung *à rebours*, as part of what seems a learnedly corrupt worship of evil and horror, I cannot but think it needful to remind readers of the sanity, the lucidity of this critic, of his constant awareness of the limits and qualities of the various forms and modes of literary expression, his constant recollection of the practice of the greatest masters and of the background of classic achievement against which, however sympathetically, all experiments must be seen.

To begin with, unlike most poets who have also been prose writers, Mr. Symons has a very just feeling for the qualities which make verse and prose what they are. Even Coleridge, the most philosophical critic we have had, could say that prose was good words in good order, and poetry the best words in the best order, though, as we hardly need to be told by Mr. Symons, there is no reason why prose should not be the best words in the best order. The history of attempts to improve the words or, more frequently, the order of the words in the Authorised Version of the Bible, in the interests of metrical form, is one long melancholy warning. What does distinguish verse from prose decisively, and the only thing that does so, is metre. All the same, verse, when it is really the vehicle of poetry,

constrains the maker of it, as Mr. Symons at various
points in his critical work has suggested, to exercise
certain preferences in the choice and the ordering
of words. It is not—an old error, triumphant in
the eighteenth century in England—that he must
as a rule prefer " poetical diction." Wordsworth
made an end of that error when he described
" poetical diction " as not the real language of men
in *any* situation, and defined the language proper
to poetry as " a selection of the real language of
men in a state of vivid sensation." But, in lyrical
poetry, at any rate, the disposition of Mr. Symons
as a poet is to use, and as a critic is to require, on
the whole a simpler vocabulary than that of prose.
Even more, in both capacities, has he preferred
for verse a simpler order, holding, and rightly,
that the inversions which are commonly thought
more legitimate in verse than in prose are far more
objectionable in verse than in prose. " The ideal
of lyrical poetry," he has said in praising lyrics
by Verlaine in which scarcely a sense of the inter-
ference of human speech remains, " is to be this
passive, flawless medium for the deeper consciousness of things, the mysterious voice of that mystery
which lies about us." He can recognise the power
and beauty of those kinds of verse in which words
assert themselves splendidly, but the ideal which
presides over his own work in verse and over his

criticism of poetry is unfavourable to the ambition of any single instrument to be heard above the rest of the orchestra.

Poetry has been defined for him, not exhaustively indeed, but in essentials, by two sentences of Joubert's : " In the style of poetry every word reverberates like the sound of a well-tuned lyre, and leaves after it numberless undulations." " Nothing is poetry which does not transport ; the lyre is in a certain sense a winged instrument." Poetry for him is a winged thing, to be captured only by means which will leave it a kind of freedom. Poetry is a wild thing, older than society and independent of it, whereas prose can have come into existence only when some social progress had been made, and needs social material for its subject matter. Prose exists to be read, poetry to be heard, if only with the ghostly voice in the mind of its solitary reader. To this day, as he says, the writing down of a poem is almost a materialisation of it.

Prose, he points out, finds its opportunities in what ties it to earth, where it can conquer new tracts and establish firm foundations. Substance, therefore, is in a way more important in prose than in verse, and unlike most poets, most writers of poetical prose, he is prepared to admit that a writer of prose may be a great writer, and yet not a great writer of prose. Instituting a very just comparison between Shakespeare and Balzac, between Lear and Père Goriot, he points out that where Lear " grows up before the mind's eye into a vast cloud and shadowy mountain of trouble, Goriot grows down and into the earth and takes root there, wrapping the dust about all his fibres." In the power of being definite, of " stationing " emotion in a firm and material way, he recognises one of the great opportunities of prose.

Understanding, then, very clearly the special capacities of verse and prose, and of each great form of both, he is in his critical demands eminently reasonable, and completely on his guard against æsthetic confusion. He is not to be duped by any irrelevant merit. Admiring, for instance, Coventry Patmore, and well aware of the subtlety, the fineness of analysis, the simplified complexity of " The Changed Allegiance," he is not to be persuaded that it should not have been done in prose ; and, admiring Meredith, remains mindful of the struggle between poetry and prose in him, and elsewhere is found contemptuously dismissing irrelevant virtues with the remark that, no matter how many figures be put on the wrong side of the zero, the sum remains zero.

All this, however, is no more than the assertion that he builds on a sound foundation. The rarer merits of his criticism come, partly, from his ability to expose himself to every kind of work as if it were his first submission to æsthetic experience. His mind is always fresh, sensitively receptive: his "nerves of delight" are always ready to respond to the faintest or the most unfamiliar stimulus. With fixed principles, which he applies with a delicate firmness to every kind of subject, he has no doctrinaire system, ready-made, into which the work of art must be forced. For while he is well aware and respectful of the great tradition, he knows that it is still in formation, and that by its very nature it must admit every vital new revelation of beauty. The greatest masters of the past, as he has reminded us in an acute, perhaps rather too hostile judgment of the work of Stephen Phillips, are akin, and yet to be studied chiefly because by their surprising differences from each other they remind us how widely we must differ from each other and from them.

He is not unwilling on occasion to consider writers in their relation to their predecessors or their fellows; he is prepared to allow that a writer or a book may have a kind of importance simply through his or its date; but he never forgets that no movement ever yet made a writer, and that what is bad art now was bad art when contemporaries admired and were influenced by it. He does not degrade criticism to the level of a history of æsthetic

H

fashions. Nor does he take any age at its own valuation, esteeming its books and writers for their fidelity to its ruling ideas, and ranking them higher or lower as they more or less fully represent their age. "Ages are all equal, but genius is always above the age," he quotes from William Blake, and it is with a special satisfaction that he makes amends to those whom their age misunderstood. As when, in what I take to be the most original critical work done in our day, he discovered the true genius of John Clare. Never was a small poet labelled with more apparent finality than Clare, who " was to have been another Burns, but succeeded only in being a better Bloomfield." And then, telling his story with a reserved, faintly ironical pathos, examining his poems with complete independence and the rarest insight, Mr. Symons recovered for us this uniquely touching poet of nature, to whom nature was a part of his home instead of his home being part of nature.

But though for Mr. Symons as for Blake the ages are all equal, he has turned away too readily, as I think, from the eighteenth century in England. It is not that I differ substantially from his rather petulant estimate of eighteenth-century poetry as a whole, or am anxious to acquire merit in quarters where, at the moment, the poetasters of that epoch are being promoted to something like eminence.

But surely there was matter there for this student of " souls in the balance," of natures troubled by what, in a self-revealing phrase, Johnson called " the hunger of the imagination which preys on life." The madness of Smart, of Collins, of Cowper, the lowered vitality of Gray and Thomson : was there not in these a hint on which this subtle exploring intelligence could have searched out the hidden, half-felt want in the life of the eighteenth century ?

Mr. Symons, however, has virtually ignored the eighteenth century, as he has ignored the English novelists, writing only some pages on Meredith and a note, but that full of penetrating criticism, on Mr. Hardy. On Italian literature he has had scarcely anything to say, dealing, except for incidental mention, only with the genius of Gabriele d'Annunzio. Of Spanish literature also he has been little moved to write, though his essay on the poetry of the mystics, containing some lovely translations, is among the finest things he has ever done. And, admiring Tolstoi as a novelist to the full, he has found Russian subjects only in Tolstoi and Gorki. French poetry after Villon and before Verlaine is to his mind on the whole too rhetorical, though in Hugo, in Baudelaire, with a really poetical rhetoric. It is only with part of French poetry that he is quite happy. The French novel, with

" Don Quixote," the first passion of his boyhood, and with the best of Tolstoi, is almost all that contents him in fiction. Balzac, Stendhal, Merimée, Flaubert, the Goncourts (whose æsthetic curiosity and general literary novelty make him perhaps too favourable a judge of their novels as such), Maupassant, Huysmans : he has written of all of them with the acutest perception. Of other French novelists also, authors of perhaps a single minor masterpiece : Benjamin Constant, whose " Adolphe " and whose " Journal " were bound to attract a critic himself expert in the dissection of love ; Murger, admirably compared by him with Bret Harte for the union of unreality with humanity; Cladel ; Laclos, whom he edited with M. Louis Thomas.*

It is, naturally, with English poetry, with what is most essentially poetic in it, that he has been most continuously happy. The evidence is to be found in every volume of his literary criticism, but is, of course, most closely concentrated into that book on *The Romantic Movement in English Poetry*, in which there is often less what we ordinarily call criticism, a numbering of the streaks of the tulip, a plucking

---

* A curious limitation in his criticism of fiction is that he seems almost indifferent to that power by which some novelists secure a rhythmical sequence of events, and is tolerant of the mechanical in plot.

apart of the petals of the rose to expose its construction, than a delicate and patient magic in response to which the flowers breathe out their inmost secrets of colour and perfume.

And in all his criticism there is a singular rightness of attitude towards literature as a thing sacred and familiar, our consecrated but daily bread, not a thing for the private enjoyment of the connoisseur or a thing to be vulgarised, but both the final luxury and the first necessity for all of us.

VII

STUDIES IN SEVEN ARTS

THROUGH the nature of the subject, but a little because Mr. Symons, expressing only part of himself in his poetry, has not quite always been able to keep the creative impulse from operating rather beside the strictly critical purpose, his criticism of pictures and music is not on the whole as inevitable as his criticism of literature. That I have already said. But I would point out, and as a conspicuous merit of the *Studies in Seven Arts* and the essays on *Plays, Acting and Music,* that he has consistently endeavoured to see each art from its own point of view. I mean that, though in writing of these arts he is sometimes, for a moment or two, fanciful rather than truly imaginative, and will now and then develop the work of art in what is not quite certainly an expansion of the artist's intention, but only a likely alternative, the development is at least in the spirit of the particular art. Mr. Symons, that is, does not go to pictures to insinuate merely literary meanings into them, he does not listen to music

102

as if it were the excuse for a defining, limiting
programme which the merely literary mind may
invent for it. He looks at pictures and at architecture, he hears music, he watches acting, and
dancing, as nearly as may be from the position of
the painter, the architect, the musician, the actor,
the dancer. He avoids—and how rare is such
avoidance!—the confusion of the arts.

In all this part of his work he has been profoundly
influenced by the salutary warning given by Walter
Pater in his essay on " The School of Giorgione."

" It is the mistake," wrote Pater, " of much
popular criticism to regard poetry, music, and
painting—all the various products of art—as but
translations into different languages of one and the
same fixed quantity of imaginative thought, sup-
plemented by certain technical qualities of colour
in painting, of sound in music, of rhythmical words
in poetry. In this way, the sensuous element in
art, and with it almost everything in art that is
essentially artistic, is made a matter of indifference ;
and a clear apprehension of the opposite principle
—that the sensuous material of each art brings
with it a special phase or quality of beauty, un-
translatable into the forms of any other, an order
of impressions distinct in kind—is the beginning
of all true æsthetic criticism."

But though Mr. Symons has never forgotten
those words of one who was, in many respects,

his master in criticism, though he has scrupulously valued in each of the arts that beauty which is yielded by its particular medium, he has been led, in thinking of art absolutely, of art conceived as independent of its material, to a paradox which Pater might not have approved, and to which we may a little demur. He has been led, that is, to the assertion of the equality of all the arts.

Now, in another writer, stimulating, suggestive, but to be taken with reserve at times, one might applaud such a paradox. For undoubtedly there has been some stupidity and snobbery in the attitude of most of us towards certain arts. Our minds have been confused by the really irrelevant consideration of immortality, or, let us put it more modestly, of durability. Because it is natural for all artists to wish to say, each of himself, *Non omnis moriar*, because some kinds of artists can and do say it, and because we ourselves, so acutely conscious that of us and our ephemeral labours there will be nothing to cast a shadow under to-morrow's sun, are heartened by the boast of immortality, we have come to esteem the arts more or less according to the hope they give of survival. But beauty is beauty, whether it be revealed for an instant in the gesture of the dancer or marmoreally preserved in the statue a sculptor makes of her. Why should we be patronising towards those arts which can offer us beauty only for the moment or few moments of its achievement ?

> *L'œuvre sort plus belle*
> *D'une forme au travail*
> *Rebelle !*

But is not the dancer's material as difficult to discipline into perfect expressiveness without irrelevancy as any ? Is the brevity of a really significant fame for the singer, the pianist, or violinist, who can no longer be heard, the actress whose last exit has been made, any sufficient reason for rating the beauty they created lower than that which lives on for us in the *vers, marbre, onyx, émail* of Gautier's demand ? Surely we need to effect here what Rémy de Gourmont would have called a dissociation of ideas, the dissociation of the idea of æsthetic value from the idea of that immortality which æsthetic value under certain conditions secures.

But to go farther, and to claim that, because beauty is always beauty, however manifested, all the arts are equal, is to imply that the material and the methods of each admit life equally. Quite obviously they do not. Music and dancing are fundamental arts because they have a full rhythmical life, to which some of the other arts attain only rather precariously; in the art of literature poetry has it, but prose only in certain special cases, and then with less inevitability. Music, again, as Pater pointed out, is the typical art because in it means and ends are identified; but music is above thought or below it; and more than any other art, for dancing produces a kind of physical intelligence in most of those who excel in the finest part of it, music can be the art of stupid, of desolatingly tedious people. Each of the arts has its special way of dealing with life, its special capacities, limitations, risks. Only literature can deal, in some degree, with everything that makes up life.

And if the arts are not all equal in their ability to render life, still less are they equally valuable in the opportunities they offer to the critic. Mr. Symons, certainly, despite the sincerity of his feeling for each, and the care with which he has looked at each from its own point of view, has been obliged to write oftener of some than of others. Of dancing, which has given him so much of the pleasure of his æsthetic life, and which, in its avoidance of emphasis, its evasive, suggestive mode of expression, its concreteness, its way of being at once more instinctive and more calculated than life can usually be, has gone so far towards embodying a certain modern ideal of art, he has written very little in critical prose. We need not be sur-

106

prised. If you speak to me of dancing, it is hardly of any particular experience of the art that I shall think, but rather of the suggestiveness of dancing in general, of its value to the imagination as a symbol of life and to the critical intelligence as the realisation of many paradoxical and necessary æsthetic requirements. Is it impudent to suppose that matters are much the same with Mr. Symons ? The influence of dancing is to be felt again and again in his work in verse and prose ; but though he has chosen as a poet to fix for us the image of certain individual dancers, La Mélinite at the Moulin Rouge, or Nini Patte-en-l'air at the Casino de Paris—

> *What exquisite indecency,*
> *Select, supreme, severe, an art !—*

the outcome for him, as a critic, is to have written on dancing in general.

As a critic of dancing, for all his tireless search after every particular excellence in London, in Paris, in Spain, he has given us the equivalent, not of his essays on Balzac or Rodin or Beethoven, but of the pages of introduction or conclusion in certain of his books : " The World as Ballet." It is otherwise that he has written of music. The pages on it in *Plays, Acting and Music* are, from the nature of the subject, less definite and final than his essays on writers, but they deal with particular composers and executants, with a keen sense of the individuality of each. The long essay, in *Studies in Seven Arts*, on " The Ideas of Richard Wagner," is a patient, highly skilled, thorough examination of those ideas, equal in merit to his examination of the ideas of Blake or of Coleridge. But of what is his finest work as a critic of music, of the strictly musical part of it, the essay on Beethoven, I am lamentably unqualified to speak. I can only record the opinion of one, entitled to an opinion, who declared to me that this essay is the profoundest and noblest thing ever written about Beethoven in English, and quote some sentences from it :

" The animal cry of desire is not in Beethoven's music. Its Bacchic leapings, when mirth abandons itself to the last ecstacy, have in them a sense of religious abandonment which belongs wholly to the Greeks, to whom this abandonment brought no sense of sin. With Christianity, the primitive orgy, the unloosing of the instincts, becomes sinful ; and in the music of Wagner's ' Venusberg ' we hear the cry of nature turned evil. . . . But to Beethoven nature was still healthy, and joy had not yet begun to be a subtle form of pain. His joy sometimes seems to us to lack poignancy, but this is because the gods, for him, have never gone into exile, and the wine-god is not a Bacchus who has

108

been in hell.   Yet there is passion in his music, a passion so profound that it becomes universal. He loves love, rather than any of the images of love.   He loves nature with the same, or with a more constant passion.   He loves God, whom he cannot name, whom he worships in no church built with hands, with an equal rapture. . . . Law, order, a faultless celestial music, alone existed for him, and these he believed to have been settled, before time was, in the heavens.   Thus his music was neither revolt nor melancholy, each an atheism ; the one being an arraignment of God and the other a denial of God."

But nowhere, so far as I can judge, has Mr. Symons shown his equity more clearly than in some of his criticism of painters and draughtsmen. The man of letters who is an art critic, with however much seriousness, only incidentally is almost bound to prefer those artists whose interest is partly literary, and the man who is curious about the subtleties of temperament is almost sure to prefer those artists who have used brush and pencil for the expression of what is not exactly the normal matter of art.

See Mr. Symons as far too many people do, and you will expect to find him limited to artists in whom there is, or into whom it is possible to read, an illegitimate interest.   Well, here is Mr. Symons understanding, praising with a just generosity, the painting of Manet, in which there is nothing but sheer good painting. Turn a page or two, and he is saying just the reverse of what, on the common conception of him, you would expect about Gustave Moreau, Puvis de Chavannes, Burne-Jones, Simeon Solomon, Rops, Beardsley ; men of genius, but of a genius for something that lies only on the fringe of art or outside it, men who have a devil or an angel. The essay on Moreau, if Mr. Symons were what he is usually taken to be, might have been an attempt to compete with Huysmans, for hardly ever has there been a painter affording so many excuses for purely literary treatment. He cries aloud to be translated back into an ornate, lustful yet frigid prose. What we actually get from Mr. Symons is a most damaging piece of criticism, with every claim submitted to the strictly pictorial test, which it cannot stand.

Yet he is very far from insensible to the peculiar attraction exercised by some of these artists. He has done, too briefly, something like justice to Simeon Solomon, who, before his collapse into using his evil, magical flame for the hasty boiling of pots, was a much more considerable painter than is usually allowed. And, in the essay on Aubrey Beardsley, the acutest and most carefully just thing ever written about that artist, he has given its full value to all that is most significant in a perversion of art carried to the point at which it becomes a paradoxical homage to that which it blasphemes. Though there was in Beardsley a certain amount of *gaminerie*, and though he condescended rather often to the kind of work in which an exquisite technique is applied to a mere caprice, the elaboration being part of the joke, he was, as Mr. Symons before anyone else and more clearly perceived, a profoundly spiritual artist in all that part of his work which most matters, and against his own will a satirist. "Beardsley's sacrifice," he rightly says, "together with that of all great decadent art, the art of Rops or of Baudelaire, is really a sacrifice to the eternal beauty, and only seemingly to the powers of evil." For evil itself can become a kind of good, "by means of that energy which, otherwise directed, is virtue, and which can never, no matter how its course may be changed, fail to retain something of its original efficacy." But with Beardsley the line, the quality of the line, is what really most concerns us, and not anything intellectual that the line was intended to express, and I find the final truth about him in these sentences by Mr. Symons:

"In those drawings of Beardsley which are grotesque rather than beautiful, in which lines begin to grow deformed, the pattern, in which now all the beauty takes refuge, is itself a moral judg-

111

ment. Look at that drawing called ' The Scarlet Pastorale.' In front, a bloated harlequin struts close to the footlights, outside the play, on which he turns his back. Beyond, sacramental candles have been lighted, and are guttering down in solitude, under an unseen wind. And between, on the sheer darkness of the stage, a bald and plumed Pierrot, holding in his vast, collapsing paunch with a mere rope of roses, shows the cloven foot, while Pierrette points at him in screaming horror, and the fat dancer turns on her toes indifferently. Need we go farther to show how much more than Gautier's meaning lies in the old paradox of ' Mademoiselle de Maupin,' that ' perfection of line is virtue ' ? That line which rounds the deformity of the cloven-footed sin, the line itself, is at once the revelation and the condemnation of vice, for it is part of that artistic logic which is morality."

I find it odd, however, that in carefully enumerating the influences on Beardsley, that of Burne-Jones, that of the Japanese, that of his senior French contemporaries, Mr. Symons should have failed to mention the influence of Greek vase designs or of Antonio Pollaiuolo.

Turn from this, to measure the breadth of this critic's sympathy, to the essay on Watts ! Yet it is with Whistler, at certain points in the lesser, in a way more characteristic part of his work, so nearly the equivalent of Mr. Symons himself, that this

112

critic is most content. Intimate his criticism always is, but here, in certain pages at any rate, he speaks almost as if he were confessing his own artistic faith in stating Whistler's, with only such critical reservations as a scrupulous artist would make in putting forth his own apology. " Exquisite and exact " he has called Whistler's world, and they are epithets for his own ; and his praise of Whistler for never forgetting that art is evocation comes home to himself, while his criticism that Whistler sometimes finds what is to the purpose by narrowing the purpose is a piece of unconscious self-criticism.

With Whistler, Duse : there was what, not exactly what we mean by acting, the stage had to give Mr. Symons for that world which he has always been building up through his poetry and many kinds of criticism. Duse, not the actress, but a woman of genius who expressed herself through acting, who came into " the movement of all the arts, as they seek to escape from the bondage of form, by a new, finer mastery of form, wrought outwards from within, not from without inwards." But again you will see the reach and suppleness and rectitude of this critic as you turn from the essay on Duse in *Studies in Seven Arts* to the pages on Sarah Bernhardt, so essentially an actress, and on Réjane, in *Plays, Acting and Music*. Merely for

I

that vivid record of the physical impression of which Hazlitt was the master the pages on Sarah Bernhardt are extraordinarily valuable. Who that ever saw her will have forgotten " the obscure sensation of peril " felt when that woman entered on the stage, or the gestures, the way of speaking verse, recorded for us by Mr. Symons ? And who will not feel that, better than when one saw Irving, one has the soul of Irving in this picture of the actor as Mephistopheles ? " With his restless strut, a blithe and aged tripping of the feet to some not quite human measure, he is like some spectral marionette, playing a game only partly his own."

Mr. Symons has said other things as admirable as that, about other actors and actresses ; he has been one of the few writers of our time, Mr. Walkley, Mr. Shaw, Mr. Max Beerbohm, Mr. Montague, and Mr. Agate being the others, who have brought to the criticism of particular plays and actors a degree of intelligence and sensibility which experience has taught us not to expect in the criticism of the theatre. But I am not at all sure that his place is not rather with those still less numerous writers who have taken us to the questions at the root of the arts of the theatre, considered abstractedly. I find, at any rate, as it seems to me, valuable and forgotten truths in his contention that an absolute criticism should admit nothing

between pantomime, in the strict and French sense
of that word, and poetic drama, and in his contention that all actors should be trained in melodrama.

In turning from all these arts to that of architecture, Mr. Symons is obliged to go to the past.
There are individual buildings in London and elsewhere which are both good and new, but there is
nothing in the world of to-day which can be called
the art of architecture. He has gone, in fact, to
the old cathedrals, to contrast Canterbury and
Cologne, that reasonable tribute to a reasonable
God, and to note how Our Lady of Amiens, though
also a daylight church, differs from Cologne.
With these pages in *Studies in Seven Arts* should be
read certain passages on "Moorish Secrets in
Spain" in the much later published *Cities and
Sea-coasts and Islands*.

"It seems to me," he writes there, "that the
architecture of the mosque is after all a more
immaterial worship of the idea of God than any
Christian architecture. Here there is invention of
pattern, into which no natural object is ever allowed to intrude, the true art for art's sake, pure
idea, mathematics, invention in the abstract; for
it is the work of an imagination intoxicated with
itself, finding beginning and end in its own formally
beautiful working out, without relation to nature
or humanity. Christianity has never accepted this

idea, indeed could not; it has always distrusted pure beauty, when that beauty has not been visibly chained to a moral."

But I could wish that Mr. Symons, never farther East than Constantinople, had found subjects in some of that Mogul architecture in India in which grandeur and an unteasing subtlety combine : the architecture at Agra, and near it at Sikandra and at Fatehpur Siki, where there is the conqueror's pride in the monument of victory, and yet everywhere the echo of the words of the inscription, " The world is a bridge, said Jesus, upon Whom be blessing, pass over it but build not upon it " ; buildings in which architecture achieves and abdicates.

He has found, however, more than enough for his purpose in London, Paris, Rome, Venice, Seville, in his delight in them, and in his distress in Moscow and in his loathing of certain aspects of Naples. I suppose only Swift and Huysmans have written with more concentrated hatred than lies in the passages of the essay on London describing the upper portion of the Edgware Road, and in some paragraphs of the essay on Naples in *Cities*. The description of the songs from which there is, or used to be, no escape in some quarters of Naples as at once " fiery and greasy " does but sum up the whole impression of all that side of Naples, with its sentimentality of the mandoline and the knife, its vivid, squalid, picturesque life. Paris, never fully dealt with by Mr. Symons, may for that reason seem to mean to him too nearly in part what it meant to the writers of the 'nineties, who fancied that ideas come to one in cafés, in part what it means to the men who droop an eyelid when announcing that they are going to Paris. It has in fact other meanings for him. But it is in Venice, in Seville, above all, though more gravely, in Rome, that he is most fully himself. It is of these three cities, and of that autumnal city of Arles, that he has written most subtly, most beautifully. Even in his prose there is no image more delicately apt than that which he has found for a garden outside Rome, with a little lake in it : " I scarcely know what it is that this unaccountable scene awaits ; but it seems to wait. Disillusioned lovers might walk there, chill even on a day of sun, seeing their past perhaps in that distant glimpse of Rome, their future in those cypress-shadowed depths, and their present in the narrow strip of brown earth between those two infinitudes." If even he has not bettered that, there is page after page of *Cities* and, especially in the English seascapes, of *Cities, Sea-coasts and Islands,* which surprises, convinces, and delights by its reflection of those aspects

in which a city or a sea-coast is exceptionally itself.
Poetry, for which we must go as a rule to the
volumes of verse, but which is sometimes juxta-
posed, completes the picture.   Now it is of Venice :

> *A city without joy or weariness,*
> *Itself beholding, from itself aloof—*

and now, in this little miracle not reprinted among
the poems, it is of Winchelsea :

> *We saw the pure lean harsh*
> *Maid's body of the marsh,*
> *Without one curve's caress*
> *In the straight daintiness*
> *Of its young frugal fine*
> *Economy of line,*
> *In faultless beauty lie*
> *Naked under the sky.*

And there is the elaborate prose miracle of the
pages on Arles, the city in which everything seems
to grow out of death and to be returning thither.
It is as if Arles itself, weary with its ancient memories,
composed in those pages its resigned, gravely
self-appreciative epitaph.

And it is in these evocations of the souls of cities,
not only because the prose is among the most

118

beautiful and personal that Mr. Symons has ever written, that his work, in a sense, culminates. The city is the final expression of man's energy. Because, as we know it, it contains so much that is stupid, ugly, and wasteful, and because its beauty, when it has any, is mostly unintended and achieved despite those who planned or allowed its growth, it scares away the timidly æsthetic. But the business of the artist is not to retire to a cloistered and merely surviving beauty : it is to find beauty wherever it exists, under whatever disguises, in however intermittent a manifestation, and not least where, though no stronger in its action than a flower, it holds its plea with the rage of contemporary civilisation. There are no cities beautiful in the sense in which the anæmic æsthete wishes them to be; the selecting and combining mind of the artist must work on the spectacle offered him by those most famous for beauty. And if there were, homage to them, to a ready-made and obvious beauty, would be too easy and too like the attitude of the susceptible cad towards women in his preference for the immediate superficial appeal. The artist in this kind of appreciation collaborates with the city he is studying, divines the gesture that ignoble traffic or some infernal improvement has spoiled, educes the soul that animates the life of the city, and says, as in the clear, sensitive, musical prose of Mr. Symons, what the city stammers all day or whispers in its dreams at night.

Mr. Symons has done all this part of his work consummately. He can see more than almost anyone with those fine eyes; his memory for things seen is extraordinary; he has his poet's imagination, his curiosity about all that is artificial, his dramatic sense of the unlimited possibilities of encounter in great cities, and he has no prejudices, not even in favour of the exotic. Knowing so many cities, he can still say that there are more beautiful women to be seen in London than anywhere else, and that the peculiar colour of London, as one looks through a vista of narrow streets towards the west at sunset, is a thing unmatched anywhere. Without prejudices, he has his significant preferences, and in making himself he has carefully submitted himself to certain cities, as to Baudelaire and Verlaine, Pater and Mallarmé, and many other artists, but other cities have meant nothing to him. To ask whether any great writer has meant nothing to him is to suggest the difference between his criticism of cities and his criticism of literature.

VIII

CONCLUSION

THE commonest and least justified derogatory criticism of Mr. Symons as a poet is that he dates, and from the little English decadence.

For a reason that will speedily appear, I should be indulging in irrelevance if I entered on a full discussion of that period, but I may at least remind the reader that, though its origins are perceptible in Swinburne, Pater, and Whistler, it can scarcely be said to have begun before 1892, and it was not long before it was checked by the social downfall of Wilde, the discontinuance of the *Yellow Book* and the *Savoy*, the deaths of Aubrey Beardsley, Ernest Dowson, Wilde himself. Give it five years or eight, it was no more than an episode ; an episode, on account of Beardsley, more important in art than in literature. How many writers were seriously, for more than a season or two, affected by it ? Not all even of the contributors to the books of the Rhymers' Club, the *Yellow Book*, the *Savoy*. The duration, the literary importance, and the influence of the decadence, with us, have all been frequently exaggerated.*

Mr. Symons for a few years seemed to have his place in it, but he had begun writing well before it developed, he did much of his finest work after it was at an end, and always he stood in an important sense aloof. With its curiosity, its concern to capture passing impressions and moods, its desire to be modern, to accept as material the artificiality of modern life, he was in sympathy ; of the cruder part of its moral error he was the severest critic. " It pleased some young men in various countries," he wrote in 1897 in the Introduction to *The Symbolist Movement in Literature*, " to call themselves Decadents, with all the thrill of unsatisfied virtue masquerading as uncomprehended vice. . . . No doubt perversity of form and perversity of matter are often found together, and, among the lesser men especially, experiment was carried far, not only in the direction of style. But a movement which in this sense might be called Decadent could but have been a straying aside from the main

* As to the moral issue, it seems to me most of the audacious young men of the period forgot that one must have a morality before one can invert it, and that the service of the Devil calls for at least as much self-control, of another kind, as the service of God.

road of literature. Nothing, not even conventional virtue, is so provincial as conventional vice ; and the desire to bewilder the middle classes is itself middle-class."

The sentences just quoted, instead of dissipating error about Mr. Symons, have quite lately been brought up against him. Well, the critic, as I said in the first pages of this book, is broader, is more nearly the whole man, than the poet in Mr. Symons, but the two coexist, and that they do so in harmony, co-operating to make his imaginative world, is his distinction. A few minor aberrations apart, they are not out of accord ; and though at one time Mr. Symons wrote some pieces of verse open perhaps to mild reproach on his own principle, he was decadent only as Baudelaire was. In the great bulk of his poetry, that is, certainly in all the finest of it, if he at all used the material offered by the decadence in its widest sense, by the sophisticated, corrupted, self-doubting life of his age, and not merely of the 'nineties, he did so otherwise than as a decadent. For he had, though not quite from the beginning, that power which, I must repeat, only Baudelaire * of the other poets

* I do not put Mr. Symons on an equality with Baudelaire. The world which is Baudelaire's is complete in his poetry ; that which Mr. Symons has made is complete only when we look at his poetry and prose together.

of the decadence has possessed ; the power of
organising his material, of making his world.   The
artificial, the ephemeral, the ambiguous, the perverse, when you consider his poetry as a whole, and
still more when you consider his entire work in
verse and prose, is not presented in isolation by
its dupe, but is related, tacitly, to the whole of a
world in which the natural, the permanent, the un-
equivocal, the normal have some, if not quite their
due place.   No doubt there is rather often in the
poetry of Mr. Symons a special relishing of various
kinds of forbidden fruit, without the irony that
attends on Baudelaire's or with less of it, and no
doubt this appreciation is not purely literary.
There is in him, at times and on his less important
side as a poet, something of that personal curiosity
about or delight in the unwholesome and perverse
which may be noted in Baudelaire and in Swinburne.   I find it much less worthy of attention
in any consideration of this writer's work as a whole
than the corresponding element in those two poets.
He gets, as a rule, less æsthetic profit out of it, even
relatively, than they did, having but little of Baudelaire's exasperated ironical idealism, and none
of Swinburne's ecstatic delight in an excuse for
the release of defiant metres.   The thing is there,
not to be ignored, to be tolerated or savoured
according to one's temperament, but it is not

124

ARTHUR SYMONS.

Photo by Elliott & Fry.

important even if you look only to his poetry,
it is corrected directly and indirectly by some of
his verse and much of his prose, and it is sheer
absurdity to fasten on it as if it were omnipresent
and supremely characteristic. It is deliberate,
but incidental; the poet is not free from it,
and doubtless would not be if he could, but
he is almost always above it, and in the end
it falls into place. You cannot, except out of
ignorance or prejudice, sink him in the little
movement of the 'nineties on a moral view of
the matter.

Well, it may be said, if his poetry does not date
morally from the little decadence, it still dates
æsthetically from the 'nineties. How far, and in
what sense? There are some pieces, chiefly in
Silhouettes and *London Nights*, which have the
dust of that period on them. But the rest? Of
most of the pieces I examined in the chapter entitled
Modern Love, you might indeed say that they
could not well have been written before 1860, and
would hardly be written, in anything like the same
way, now. But that is dating only as much as
Tennyson, Browning, Arnold, Rossetti, Morris,
Swinburne, and Meredith date, from an age, not
from a fashion. Of certain other pieces, impressions of things seen, we might, similarly, admit
that they date as Whistler and Dégas do. There

can here be no implications that they were in a
mode which means nothing to another generation.
But I have something in reserve.

Will anyone tell me how to date a dozen of the
best songs and brief lyrics made by Mr. Symons?
They connect him on the one hand with the Elizabethans, and on the other with Verlaine, and are
his own. They belong, beyond possibility of
question, to the eternal now of our poetry. Take
one of the slenderest of them, a song for the lute,
written for Madame Dolmetsch. It is, with reason,
in one respect archaic, but unobtrusively; and it
is, in another respect, unobtrusively modern.
Take a lyric like the beautiful " Rest," which was
written in 1899, at Prague :

> *The peace of a wandering sky.*
> *Silence, only the cry*
> *Of the crickets, suddenly still,*
> *A bee on the window-sill,*
> *A bird's wing, rushing and soft,*
> *Three flails that tramp in the loft,*
> *Summer murmuring*
> *Some sweet, slumberous thing,*
> *Half asleep ; but thou, cease,*
> *Heart, to hunger for peace,*
> *Or, if thou must find rest,*
> *Cease to beat in my breast.*

Conclusion

With what passing mode does that conform?
" The Crying of Water," written a year later, and
its companion piece, " The Crying of the Earth,"
written in 1906, have a music in part, perhaps,
learned from Mr. Yeats, but each has qualities
proper to Mr. Symons, and the former, at any rate,
is a thing of rare poignancy. " Wind in the
Valley," if you like, has slightly Meredithian
imagery :

> *Hands of wind are at the doors,*
> *Feet of wind upon the roof,*
> *Wind with dragon voices roars*
> *Blindly, trumpeting aloof.*
>
> *Mouths of wind at all the cracks*
> *Whistle through the walls, and, hark !*
> *Lashes clang on leaping backs*
> *Of the horses of the dark.*

But it suggests neither discipleship nor date. In
such things, in " Wind at Night," in " Night,"
in " Think of nothing but the day," in " Veneta
Marina," in " Her eyes say Yes, her lips say No,"
in " The Barrel-Organ," something that it has
always been natural to do in English lyric verse
is done in a way that is both old and new.

The diction, as always in the verse of Mr. Symons

127

but especially in the songs and concentrated lyrics, is pure ; the construction of the sentences of a distinguished simplicity ; the writing delicately taut, the music coaxed out of words instead of extorted from them. There are no tricks, of the 'nineties or of any other period ; there are no baits for the public of that day or any. Simplicity, in the fine meaning of the word, can hardly go farther than in " Montserrat," which is one of its author's chief successes in this kind, and which relies so little on verbiage that it actually contains only three words of more than one syllable. Brevity, with completeness, can hardly go farther than in :

Gold and blue of a sunset sky,
Bees that buzz with a sleepy tune,
A lowing cow and a cricket's cry,
Swallows flying across the moon.

Swallows flying across the moon,
The trees darken, the fields grow white ;
Day is over, and night comes soon :
The wings are all gone into the night.

It is so nearly nothing ; only, the last line, in itself nearly nothing, has stirred something in the mind, and this tiny poem has become the expression of finality, as if it were about the last sunset our eyes

128

will see. There is an earlier, equally slight poem
by Mr. Symons, a mere impression of the Temple
by moonlight, which ends with another kind of
simple magic :

> *O the refrain of years on years*
> *'Neath the weeping moon !*

These last are very minor miracles, but they are
miracles, not effects the knack of which was learn-
able in the 'nineties. And it is with the songs and
certain of the shortest lyrics, in which Mr. Symons
is obviously dependent on the sheer poetry in him
for every second of the minute or two they take in
the reading, that the hostile critic can most easily
be refuted.

It is on these things that the anthologist of the
future will most probably seize. They are the most
indisputable part of his poetic achievement, as the
often slightly perverse hymns of that " religion
of the eyes " which he practised are the most
novel part of it, and as the poems of modern love
are psychologically the most important. Mr.
Symons, as I suppose, will fare at the hands of the
anthologist much as Donne does. To the reader
of anthologies, Donne is the singer of some five
or six songs, in which a new intellectual subtlety
has come into the Elizabethan music ; the greater

K   129

Donne, troubled with lust and religion, tortured by his own passionate casuistry, is unknown. And I dare say that fifty or a hundred years hence Mr. Symons will be for most people the writer of certain songs, which they may think were rivalled in their age, in the essential singing quality, only by those of Mr. Robert Bridges.

But this book is mainly a protest against the anthologists' way of dealing with its subject. As I endeavoured to show at the very outset, it is necessary, if we are to understand Mr. Symons, to take all his work into consideration, with careful regard to his single, sustained ambition.

Poetry, Mr. Symons has said, begins where prose ends, and it is at its peril that it begins sooner. An obvious truth, but one useless to a writer who, having prose interests as well as poetical, has not the prose which can push its frontier right up to that of poetry. Most English poets have been good, some have been great prose writers, and many have flung fragments of scarcely disguised poetry into their prose, but hardly any have seriously tried to train prose to conquer, by its own methods, the borderlands of poetry. The prose of Swinburne, for instance, though disfigured by several kinds of excess and some irritating tricks, is at its best a magnificent thing, but it is only a means for the declamation of passionate opinions, and it is impossible that it should convey any really intimate part of its author's thought and feeling. But what Mr. Symons writes is the prose of the confessional, an intimate, scrupulous, patient, hushed prose, coming from the æsthetic conscience. It can do, in his eventual command of it, much that descriptive and meditative poetry can do; it can unpack his heart almost as completely as a sequence of sonnets ; and it has to resign in favour of verse only when there is need of a more concentrated, a more regularly rhythmed, a more releasing means of expression than prose can ever be. There is for him no temptation to let poetry begin before it must. Prose will serve him to the very limit of its province.

His verse, then, is his means of dealing with the precious residue of experience which prose cannot treat. Is it always the gainer for that ? In logic, it should be, but art is perhaps not less free from logic than life, and I am not sure that something has not been lost. Was it quite inevitable, or is it part of the price of the prose writer's success, that the poet should be so considerably less than the whole man, so self-regarding in what the prose writer's theory and practice have left him for principality ? I do not know. But I do know the prose writer's success has had its dangers. For what Mr. Symons has written in prose, some few score pages excepted, is criticism, and on a more liberal interpretation all his prose is critical. Well, as Mr. Symons himself has pointed out, " for the critic to aim at making literature is to take off something from the value of his criticism as criticism." Yet it is not quite that danger which I have in mind. Rather, the danger that a writer whose strictly creative work is narrowed, partly by natural limitations, partly by theoretical restraints, may become creative in his criticism in not the most legitimate way.

In dealing with literature Mr. Symons never, I think, falls a victim to this impulse. It is otherwise, now and then, in his criticism of pictures, plays, music, dancing, and in his studies of cities and seascapes. There, at times, though, one gratefully admits, infrequently and but for a paragraph or two at the most, he may be found simply the recorder of a personal reaction or reverie, which you may share and I may not, the reporter of an impression to which there are alternatives. I am far from saying that it will not have value even for those who cannot share it. Every response of so sensitive and distinguished a mind to beauty is deserving of respectful attention. But, having lost inevitability, it misses the dual success of his literary criticism. Yet its failure, in the lower part of the task, will not be useless to the reader whom it reminds of this writer's real aim.

*   *   *

To ask of Shakespeare or Balzac why they create is as if one asked of the sun why it shines. In the great masters creation is out of an imperious law of their being, and their worlds are cast off with an eager, ample energy that has and requires no stimulus beyond the joy of power in its exercise. But there are other artists, in whom the creative impulse is quickened by something personal, and of them we may well ask why they create. The quickening with Mr. Symons comes from a troubled sense of the conditions under which we live, with our one opportunity, and that an opportunity, in the absence of knowledge what it is for, bound to be more or less wasted.

Mr. Symons has always been haunted by that sentence of Victor Hugo's, "we are all of us condemned to death, with indefinite reprieves." The inevitability of death, which, luckily, seems no more than a lugubrious generalisation without reference to us ourselves as we go about our own business, came home to him early, as he has told us in some substantially autobiographical pages :

"I remember once in church, as I was looking earnestly at the face of a child for whom I had a boyish admiration, that the thought suddenly shot into my mind : ' Emma will die, Emma will go to heaven, and I shall never see her again.' I shivered all through my body, I seemed to see her vanishing away from me, and I turned my eyes aside, so that I could not see her. But the thought gnawed at me so fiercely that a prayer broke out of me, silently, like sweat : ' O God, let me be with her ! O God, let me be with her ! ' When I came out into the open air, and felt a cold breeze on my forehead, the thought had begun to release its hold on me, and I never felt it again, with that certainty, but it was as if a veil had been withdrawn for an instant, the veil which renders life possible, and, for that instant, I had seen."

" To live through a single day," he has written elsewhere, in the concluding pages of *The Symbolist Movement in Literature*, " to live through a single day with that overpowering consciousness of our real position, which, in the moments in which alone it mercifully comes, is like a blinding light or the thrust of a flaming sword, would drive any man out of his senses."

There is in this, as he himself has explained, no cowardice. The torture is in realising that the certainty for which the soul cries out can be attained only when it is too late. We have only one question to ask of death, the meaning of life, and the answer

134

can only be useless when, life being over, we
receive it. If we receive it at all ! For it is a
further part of this torture to reflect that there may
be no answer, death itself, as in his impressive,
shudderingly felt morality, *The Fool of the World*,
being a dupe.

Only Death knows, only Death can
Speak the whole truth of death to man.
O Death, Death kind and piteous,
Have pity and tell the truth to us.

    DEATH (rising).   *Shall the seven bells of folly know*
Pity, that lead me where I go ?

    (She throws down the staff of bells.)

Have pity, all ye that draw breath,
O men, have pity upon Death.
The bells that weigh about my brows,
And ring all flesh into my house,
Are a fool's witless bells ;

    (She throws down the cap of bells.)

                             I lead

The dance of fools, a fool indeed ;
And my hands gather where they find,
For I am Death, and I am blind.

    (She takes off the mask and falls on her
       knee.)

One to whom such thoughts come must needs contrive for himself some barrier or some distraction, and when Mr. Symons entitles a section of his poems, " Guests "—

> *Then, as my neighbour thought and I sit down . . .*
> *Each plots to call in guests, if guests there be*
> *That would sit down between my thought and me—*

he is hinting to us part of the reason for his activity in verse and prose alike. It concerns us to know that reason.   For, however much we may appreciate the faces and temperaments and works of art and cities that he will thus call up out of memory, we shall not understand him till we have grasped the motive of this hospitality. Yet the desire, the aching need of distraction, is but the motive of his weaker moments. To become absorbed in something else may be the only counsel which a mind tortured by a thought can give itself or receive, but guests come and go, provide only a temporary relief, and the mind yearns for permanent relief, and cannot be content with hours of mere distraction. It requires that in which it can be absorbed wholly, without limit except that set by the intensity of its desire for absorption ; it requires the absolute.

It can find that only in religion, or love, or art, each a faith, an affirmation that, beyond the reach of reason, there exists something perfect and immortal. But as there have been saints whose achievement was mystical union with God, their good works being to them but incidental, and lovers whose achievement has been the imaginative fusion of their love with that which moves the sun and stars, their service to each other being in their own eyes subsidiary, so there have been artists whose achievement has been the relation of this world to a world of their own making, their success in producing particular works of art being no more to them than the saint's in a good act, or the lover's in a courtesy to his mistress.

It is impossible that such artists should be contented specialists. In each department of the life they would make over again into its divine likeness they may be as fastidious as you like, but as between department and department they must not choose : it is a whole world that they have to make. Their fastidiousness will be wise in so far as they select for transformation nothing that does not accord with their principles, which are to unify the world they are making. Their greatness will depend on their power of inclusion : of co-ordinating, with their few principles, God's plenty, which coheres through an infinite number of principles.

The world which Mr. Symons has made is not a large one. It is full of beautiful things, transformed in a way proper to him,

> *Beautiful things of earth, but changed,*
> *Made pallid, delicate, estranged*
> *From the gold light, the glittering air.*

As a world, it is open to the criticism that it is inhabitable, for any length of time, by no one except its author. It has been made by a lonely man, in self-defence and for consolation, with a kind of secrecy as he went about what seemed the ordinary business of the poet and the critic, and after all it leaves him unconsoled and in peril from himself. He is like a man who should choose to dwell in a house filled with things which have intimate associations and meanings, without the relief of indifferent things. He has done his work, the one work at which he has laboured under many disguises, in a sense too well, has made his world too exclusively of things that have an oppressively personal significance, that remind him too persistently of his identity. Having both gloried in and cried out against the narrowing

138

of thought and passion to the limits of his own personality—

> *If I could know but when and why*
> *This piece of thoughtless dust begins*
> *To think, and straightway I am I,*
> *And these bright hopes and these brave sins,*
> *That have been freer than the air,*
> *Circle their freedom with my span,*

he escapes into a world still more personal, to cherish his identity still more and to cry out against it even more vehemently :

> *I know I am myself mine own*
> *Chimaera, chained, famished, alone,*
> *Whose anger heartens him afresh*
> *To feed upon his very flesh,*
> *Till anguish bid delight to pause,*
> *And I must suffer him because*
> *Until the hour when God shall send*
> *Suddenly the reluctant end*
> *He with my breath must draw his breath.*
> *O bondslave, bondslave unto death,*
> *Might I but hope that death should free*
> *This self from its eternity !*

With a more widely ranging critical intelligence than any other writer of our time, with a more

truly catholic receptiveness, he is more shut up
with himself than any other, with a subtler pride
in his loneliness, and, in his infrequent welcome
to ordinary human feeling, a more delicately
pathetic hospitality.

BIBLIOGRAPHICAL NOTE

I. WORKS BY ARTHUR SYMONS

(The titles of volumes of verse are given in italics)

1. An Introduction to the Study of Browning. 1886. Revised Edition, 1906.
2. *Days and Nights.* 1889.
3. *Silhouettes.* 1892. Revised edition, 1896.
4. *London Nights.* 1894. Revised edition, 1896.
5. Studies in Two Literatures. 1897.

   (The volume of the Collected Works bearing this title does not reproduce the contents of the book as issued in 1897. Certain essays were transferred to " Studies in Prose and Verse," in 1904, certain others to " Studies in the Elizabethan Drama," in 1920.)
6. *Amoris Victima.* 1897.
7. Aubrey Beardsley. 1898. Revised edition, 1905.

   (Incorporated in " Studies in Seven Arts " in the Collected Works.)
8. The Symbolist Movement in Literature. 1899.

(Incorporated, unfortunately, in " Studies in Two Literatures " in the Collected Works, where it has some irrelevant, though in itself valuable, matter in the context.)

9. *Poems.* (First collected edition, two volumes.) 1902.
(Reprints only a few of the pieces in *Days and Nights*.)

10. Plays, Acting and Music. 1903. Revised edition, 1909.

11. Cities. 1903.
(The essay on Seville was subsequently transferred to " Cities and Sea-coasts and Islands," 1917.)

12. Studies in Prose and Verse. 1904.
(Reproduces some of the essays in the original volume of " Studies in Two Literatures " and the Prefaces to the revised editions of *Silhouettes* and *London Nights*.)

13. *A Book of Twenty Songs.* 1905.
(Reproduced in *The Fool of the World*.)

14. Spiritual Adventures. 1905.

15. *The Fool of the World, and Other Poems.* 1906.

16. Studies in Seven Arts. 1906.
(The volume so entitled in the Collected Works incorporates " Aubrey Beardsley.")

17. William Blake. 1907.

18. Cities of Italy. 1907.

142

19. The Romantic Movement in English Poetry. 1909.
20. *Knave of Hearts.* 1913.
21. Figures of Several Centuries. 1916.
22. *Tragedies.* 1916.
    (" The Death of Agrippina," " Cleopatra in Judæa," " The Harvesters.")
23. *Tristan and Iseult.* 1917.
24. Cities and Sea-coasts and Islands. 1917.
    (This volume includes " London : A Book of Aspects," previously issued privately, the essay on Seville from " Cities," and the study of Campoamor from "Studies in Prose and Verse.")
25. Baudelaire. 1920.
26. *Love's Cruelty.* 1923.
    (This list takes no account of American issues of the work of this writer, among which may be mentioned " Dramatis Personae," or of minor issues like " The Café Royal and Other Essays," lately published in London by Mr. Beaumont.
    The works of Mr. Symons, originally issued by Leonard Smithers, J. M. Dent, Heinemann, Constable, and others, are now, apparently with some omissions and additions, being issued in a collected edition by Martin Secker, for which see below.)

27. The Collected Works of Arthur Symons. 1924.
(In 16 volumes, limited to 550 ordinary and
100 special sets; only six volumes so far
issued.)

II. WORKS TRANSLATED BY ARTHUR SYMONS

1. Gabriele d'Annunzio: The Child of Pleasure.
(Only the verses translated by Arthur
Symons.) 1898.
2. Gabriele d'Annunzio: The Dead City. 1900.
3. Gabriele d'Annunzio: Gioconda. 1901.
4. Gabriele d'Annunzio: Francesca da Rimini.
1902.
5. Verhaeren: Les Aubes. 1898.
6. Zola: L'Assommoir. 1894.
7. Baudelaire: Works. 1925.
(Includes the translation of the Prose Poems
issued earlier.)

III. WORKS EDITED OR INTRODUCED BY ARTHUR SYMONS

1. Addison, Joseph: Sir Roger de Coverley, etc.
With a Preface. 1905.
2. St. Augustine: The Confessions. Edited, with
an Introduction. 1898.
3. Blind, Mathilde: A Selection from the Poems
of Mathilde Blind. Edited. 1897.

4. Blind, Mathilde: The Poetical Works of Mathilde Blind. Edited. 1900.

5. Brontë, Emily: Poems, With an Introduction (and a poem). 1906.

6. Browning, Robert: Pippa Passes. With an Introduction. 1906.

7. Byron: Poems. With an Introduction. 1904.

8. Choderlos de Laclos: Poesies. Publiées par A. Symons et L. Thomas.

9. Clare, John: Poems. Edited. With an Introduction. 1908.

10. Coleridge: Poems. Selected and arranged. With an Introduction. 1905.

11. Coleridge: Biographia Literaria. Selected and arranged. With an Introduction. 1906.

12. Day, John: The Parliament of Bees, etc. Edited. 1887.

13. Dowson, Ernest: Poems. With a Memoir. 1905.

14. Flaubert, Gustave: Salammbo. With an Introduction. 1908.
(See also " French Novels of the Nineteenth Century.")

15. French Novels of the Nineteenth Century. Preface to each Volume. 1901, etc.

16. Hunt, Leigh: Essays. Edited. 1887.

17. Keats: Poems. Selected, with an Introduction. 1907.

L

18. Landor, W. S. The Hellenics and Gebir. Edited. 1907.
19. Massinger: Plays. Edited. 1887.
20. Maupassant: Boule de Suif. With an Introduction. 1899.
21. Merimée, P.: Colomba and Carmen. With a critical Introduction. 1902.
22. Murger, H.: The Latin Quarter. (Vie de Bohème.) 1908.
   (See also " French Novels of the Nineteenth Century.")
23. Naidu, Sarojini: The Golden Threshold. Introduction. 1905.
24. Pater, Walter: Portraits Imaginaires. Introduction d'A. Symons. 1899.
25. Poe : The Lyrical Poems. Introduction. 1906.
26. Shakespeare: King Henry V. Facsimile of the First Quarto. Introduction. 1886.
27. Shakespeare: King Henry V. Facsimile of the Third Quarto. Introduction. 1886.
28. Shakespeare: Titus Andronicus. Introduction. 1886.
29. Shakespeare: Venus and Adonis. Introduction. 1886.
30. Shakespeare: Cymbeline. Introduction. 1906.

Mr. Symons also contributed Introductions to the selections from various poets in " Poets and Poetry of the Nineteenth

Century," selected by A. H. Miles, notably to the selections
from Christina Rossetti and Swinburne. To the "Ency-
clopædia Britannica," eleventh edition, he contributed an
important article on Thomas Hardy. To the "Cambridge
History of English Literature" he contributed the chapter
on the joint work of Middleton and William Rowley,
analysing the contribution of each with exceptional skill.

IV. ANTHOLOGIES EDITED BY ARTHUR SYMONS

1. A Sixteenth Century Anthology. 1903.
2. A Book of Parodies. 1903.
3. A Pageant of Elizabethan Poetry. 1906.

V. CRITICISMS OF ARTHUR SYMONS

There has not so far appeared any comprehensive study
of the work of this writer. A selection from his poems—
"*Poésies*," Bruges, 1907—edited and for the most part
translated by M. Louis Thomas, contains an essay on him
by that writer. A brochure by Mr. Blaikie Murdoch—
"Arthur Symons"—appeared some years ago, but was too
brief, partial, and Scottish. Almost the only thoroughly
intelligent review of his collected "Poems," 1902 (really,
end of 1901), with which I am acquainted was printed in the
Athenæum early in 1902. Walter Pater's notice of his first
volume of verse has been reprinted as an introduction to
the recent reissue of *Days and Nights*, as a separate volume,
by Mr. Martin Secker. A review of "The Romantic Movement in English Poetry" by Mr. Runciman, the musical
critic, in the *Saturday Review*, 1909, is worth looking at, and
perhaps I may mention my own article on Mr. Symons in

the *Saturday Review* last year, ostensibly a review of the first volumes of his Collected Works. With the exception of an unsympathetic article by Mr. Francis Gribble, in the *Fortnightly Review*, 1908, it was the first attempt, so far as I know, to discuss his general attitude.

His earlier work in verse was considered in the late Mr. William Archer's "Poets of the Younger Generation," a quarter of a century ago. He has also been dealt with in relation to his contemporaries, in Mr. Holbrook Jackson's useful book on "The Eighteen Nineties," and in Mr. Burdett's recent book on "The Beardsley Period." Mr. Burdett falls into the old error about the poems, but is most intelligently generous in dealing with the criticism.

Some scattered opinions about his work and literary personality may be found in a letter written by Lionel Johnson to Katharine Tynan, and quoted in the introduction by Mr. Ezra Pound to Lionel Johnson's Collected Poems; in Mr. George Moore's autobiographical trilogy; and in the reminiscences of Mr. Yeats. Sir Arthur Quiller-Couch managed to leave him out of the "Oxford Book of English Verse;" he also left out Lionel Johnson and Ernest Dowson. The only anthologist who seems to have understood what he had to deal with, Mr. St. John Lucas, besides including some pieces in "The Rose-Winged Hours," acknowledged obligations to the "Pageant of Elizabethan Poetry," edited by Mr. Symons, calling it the faultless issue of an impeccable taste. As far as I am aware, none of his prose has been included in any anthology.

Printed in Great Britain by Hazell, Watson & Viney, Ld.,
London and Aylesbury.